Tripping 1975

Falling in Love One Country at a Time

Marshall Hockett

With
Debbie Hockett

DMH Press
San Diego, CA

Copyright © 2020 Marshall Hockett

All rights reserved.

No part of this publication may be reproduced, stored in or introduced into a retrieval system, or transmitted, in any form, or by any means (electronic, mechanical, photocopying, recording, or otherwise), without the prior permission of the publisher except in the case of brief quotations embodied in critical articles and review. Requests for permission should be directed to DMH Press.

Book Cover and Interior Design by Monkey C Media
Copyediting by All My Best
Proofread by Adrienne Moch
All photos courtesy of Marshall Hockett

First Edition
Printed in the United States of America

ISBN: 978-1-7331445-0-6

Library of Congress Control Number: 2019913624

Contents

Prologue		1
Germany/Luxembourg	March 6, 1975	3
France	March 8—April 4, 1975	7
Amsterdam	April 8–11, 1975	25
France	April 14–18, 1975	33
Spain	April 20—June 3, 1975	41
France	June 4–10, 1975	71
Great Britain	June 11—July 5, 1975	83
Scotland and Wales	July 8–30, 1975	95
Germany and Switzerland	August 6–15, 1975	115
Austria	August 19–30, 1975	125
Yugoslavia	September 3–7, 1975	133
Yugoslavia and Bulgaria	September 10–13, 1975	139
Turkey	September 14—October 17, 1975	147
Greece	October 18–27, 1975	163
Egypt	November 1–11, 1975	169
Crete	November 4–16, 1975	181
Greece	November 18—December 8, 1975	185
Israel	December 12–18, 1975	199
Italy	December 25, 1975—January 20, 1976	207
Germany	January 22—February 8, 1976	223
Paris	February 12—March 7, 1976	231
Epilogue		243
The Books I Read Along the Way		245

Prologue

That night in early 1975, Debbie and I were very excited. We had sold our cars and gotten our passports, vaccines, new clothes, maps, etc. Leaving in less than a week, we were ready for our one-year trip to Europe.

We were out to dinner with our good friends, Jim and Marian Malkus. As I recall, Marian was concerned about our safety traveling all over Europe and living in a van. After all, neither Debbie nor I had ever even camped a day in our lives. Jim thought we were "gutsy" to leave our jobs, living off money we had wisely saved but now apparently were willing to risk all, with no assurance of jobs when we got back.

My parents knew we were crazy. After putting me through college at Stanford and then law school, they were expecting my legal career to be off and running, rather than my running away to Europe for a year. My mother was positive we would be "back in a month." My dad was concerned that I would be setting back my career as an attorney. However, Debbie and I knew this would be the last chance in our lives to really live and experience what the world was offering. We both felt that children and jobs could wait at least a year.

Back to the dinner—I was totally surprised when Marian handed me a red bound book that was completely blank. She looked at us and said, "Fill it up, and be totally honest." Her second wish was that she must be the first to read it. Up to that point, I had never even considered keeping a journal of the journey ahead. I agreed to her conditions. Marian beamed and we toasted the future.

Upon our return, she was the first to read the journal. What once was an empty book was now filled with wonderful adventures. She said she loved it and that others would also. Unfortunately, Marian did not make it—she lost her battle with cancer. Her bright light is gone, but not her spirit or her enduring influences on her many friends.

Of course, once our yearlong adventure had come to an end, a new one awaited us. The journal sat forgotten in my library while I got busy building that career. Recently, a court clerk and I were talking about travel. She thought I should perhaps write a book about our experiences. Something clicked. I looked at the clerk and said, "I did!" Afterwards, I gave her the red bound book. She then read the journal and soon it was being passed throughout the courthouse.

Marian, this one is for you.

—Marshall

Germany/ Luxembourg

March 6, 1975

March 6, 1975

10:00 p.m.
Luxembourg

What makes two kids give up well-paying jobs and a beautiful penthouse apartment overlooking Mission Bay in San Diego to travel eight thousand miles to the heart of Europe? A dream—one that began in 1968 when I studied at Stanford's campus in Britain. I swore then that I would come back and really see this place called Europe, but only if I could spend the proper amount of time and only if I had the proper "security" to put me at ease during the trip. So off to law school and my first legal job at Legal Aid Society of San Diego—which I left just seven days ago.

I probably would have been here a year ago, but I met and fell in love with the prettiest court clerk in San Diego, Debbie. Two weeks after I met her, I knew I wasn't going without her.

So, we're here! We arrived this morning at 4:00 a.m. after a plane flight I was beginning to think would never end. We landed in Frankfurt, Germany, and after going through a very easy customs check we took a very nice, warm, and slow train to Luxembourg via Mainz, Wiensbaden, and Koblenz. Beautiful scenery lined the route most of the way, with several castles overlooking various rivers. But we were both so tired that the second we arrived, we got a taxi and headed straight for the Hotel Molitor on Avenue de la Liberte. We sacked out from 1:00 p.m. to 8:00 p.m. and then went out for a pizza dinner I wouldn't serve the family dog. But the wine was excellent, our spirits are high, and we are looking forward to a most exciting trip.

We pick up the camper van tomorrow.

France

March 8—April 4, 1975

March 8, 1975

10:00 p.m.
Paris

Tonight, I am writing you from one of Europe's lousiest hotel rooms. It has no heat; however, there are plenty of roaches. I'd say it is about 9 feet by 18 feet, with windows overlooking a very noisy street.

You're probably asking yourself how we happened to find such a paradise. Well, it wasn't easy.

It all started yesterday when we bought the van. I tried to get the van to the gas pumps, but failed to get her to start. Debbie had problems, too, so the salesman took it to the pump for us.

Then Debbie took over the driving after promising to give me lessons on stick-shift driving. Man, what an ego deflator.

We bought some camping gear from an old fellow about a hundred years old. I really liked him; however, I liked him less when we discovered that we had been shortchanged about forty dollars. I don't think it was on purpose, just a funny old fellow who couldn't add right.

We spent that night camping at Dommeldonge, Luxembourg. Have you ever wondered what a sardine feels like when it's in the can in your refrigerator? Yep, Debbie and I found out. But, despite the rain and cold and the thousand-hour night, Debbie and I were up at 7:00 a.m. and off to Paris.

We stopped at Verdun and saw the memorial, etc.—longest battle of WW I. We drove through the beautiful scenery with great expectations, as we knew that the camping in Paris had to be better than last night.

Naturally, since I still can't drive the van, Debbie drove the whole way. And once arriving in Paris, well—it was sort of like being on all the rides at Disneyland at the same time with hundreds of people trying to drive into you. But, I want you to know, I was right there helping Debbie out by looking through my fingers from time to time and screaming that we were about to die.

Yet Debbie pulled us through like a champ. Not a mark on either of us or the van—however, neither of us can sleep tonight. We searched for the campground for about an hour, following signs that led us to just about everyplace else. Finally, we found our "open all year round" campground. Unfortunately, it looked like no one had been there for ten years. Completely deserted.

Well, then it was back across the city to our standby; the hotel I stayed in as a student in 1968. From the graffiti on the windows, I think we missed its demise by about a year. Next, we carefully searched the surrounding area. Actually, we got lost and stopped at the first available parking space. From there it was an easy hour and half trying to visit every filled hotel within walking distance. Finally, we settled on this paradise—the first room available.

A somewhat humorous event occurred in our hotel on our first night in Paris. In the middle of the night, there was a sudden, huge commotion. Since the walls were paper-thin, you could hear every word. Apparently, the gentleman who was yelling and screaming had a dispute as to the status of the relationship between him and the woman he was addressing. Basically, the gentleman was seeking a credit for services to be performed immediately as he was without funds. He assured her that he was a man of honor and he would raise the funds before noon tomorrow.

The young lady's position was quite simple: The gentleman had not paid on several different occasions. Then, all hell broke loose. Screaming, name calling, and kicking in doors. It was a wonderful introduction to Paris.

After consulting with Debbie, we decided to put the bed in front of the door—after all, the door didn't have a lock. The next morning, the woman running the hotel was bright and chipper. She asked if we would be spending another night. We said that, unfortunately, our plans simply wouldn't allow it, and we departed.

Naturally, all the cards are going home saying, "Having a great time!" and we really are—well, sort of, anyway.

March 10, 1975

Midnight
Paris

We searched everywhere for two days trying to find a nice place to stay for a month and finally settled on Hotel Daguerre.

It's fairly cheap, but our room is clean and it overlooks a backyard rather than a busy street. Unfortunately, it has no heat and we are seven flights up without an elevator. Debbie described the place in her log as "charming"; however, I really wouldn't know. By the time I get to the top of 115 steps, I'm so tired and dizzy I couldn't care less what it looks like.

The other side of the room had much more ambiance.

Last night, we ate in a small hole-in-the-wall type place that I discovered as a student seven years ago. It's an Algerian place that serves couscous. What a pleasant surprise to see that it was still there!

And, still being run by the same old fellow! Since you sit wherever there is a seat available, we ate next to a Scotsman and a Frenchman. The Scot said this was going to be the first and last time he tried couscous. However, I find that with a couple of glasses of wine, it's great—and also, it's cheap!

We walked down St. Michael Boulevard, and I found things pretty much as I remembered them in the old days, except twice the price. It's so nice to walk around and watch the cars banging into each other rather than participating. Debbie and I agreed that one of the worst jobs in the world would be a driving instructor in Paris. It's the only job I know with a life expectancy of three days.

March 14, 1975

4:00 p.m.
Paris

Things are going well. It's still rainy and cold. However, Debbie and I are well settled into our room and it has become a nice little haven for us to run to after wearing ourselves out at museums.

One of the maids brings us our breakfast (*le petit-dejeuner*) around 9:00 a.m. As it's a continental breakfast, it consists solely of two rolls and tea—oops, nearly forgot—also about three sips of something close to orange juice. Breakfast got later and later until we started tipping the maid.

We've seen the usual sights: Napoleon's Tomb (where's Josephine?), Eiffel Tower, Louvre, etc. However, my favorite spot in Paris is the Jeu de Paume, a small museum close to the Louvre that has a great collection of the impressionist painters—Monet, Degas, Morisot, Pissaro, Renoir—the list goes on. We've spent almost two hours there already and haven't gotten to the second floor!

Last night we ate dinner with Jake and Jaqui, a couple we know in San Diego who are spending a few days in Paris. We ate in Le Procope, a fun little place established in 1686 and supposedly frequented by Napoleon, Ben Franklin, and the like. The food was excellent—escargot, roast duck with cherries, cheese, wine, and a banana split. Eating is a real event in this city—when you go into a nice restaurant, it's expected that you are there for the evening. For that reason, the atmosphere is very relaxed, nothing is rushed, and the food is prepared with great care.

Marie Antoinette, March 14, Paris.

Louis XIV, March 14.

Paris has a first-class subway system called the Metro. It takes you anywhere in town for twenty cents. Considering the nightmare on the roads above you, it's cheap at four times the price.

March 18, 1975

7:00 p.m.
Paris

It snowed last night and early this morning! It is so cold in this room, I am seriously thinking about subletting part of it to store meat. Anyway, after an hour of running around the room to warm up, we took off for the Metro (Pont de Sevres) and then caught the bus to Versailles.

Versailles was just as I remembered it—very large, very ornate, and this time, a lot of snow. Although we went there by ourselves, Debbie and I slipped into an English guided tour of the palace. One thing had changed however: history. This time, the guide had Marie Antoinette going out on the balcony alone, facing the mob from Paris. She even had the courage to "smile them into silence." The last time I was here, Louis XVI addressed the crowd, with Marie hiding in the room behind him. I never realized how powerful the women's lib movement is—it changed history. But, as usual, no one alive knows what really happened. However, who really cares—the stories are great.

We've tromped around the city several days now—went by the Jeu de Paume again and bought three prints, saw the Rodin Museum, and took a picture of Debbie next to *The Thinker*.

I am still amazed at how nice the people of Paris have been to us. Several reasons I suspect. Not nearly the great number of us that used to be here (Americans, that is) and the mighty dollar has been humbled.

But, where Americans have left off, the Japanese have certainly taken over well. I'd wager there was more Japanese spoken at Versailles today than all the other languages put together. Additionally, the shy and retiring Oriental is gone with the ten-cent Coke—they're in there pushing and shoving with the best of the tourists. Looks like we did a splendid job of "Americanizing" them after the war.

March 22, 1975

4:00 p.m.
Paris

Well folks, it was the crime of the century. A real professional job.

Yep, as Debbie and I returned from our walk down the Champs-Elysees and visiting the Pantheon, we walked down Rue Froidevaux to make the regular check on the van. As we approached, I noticed that all of the curtains had been shut! What a sinking feeling when you know someone has broken into your car or house. Anyway, we rushed up and discovered that whoever it was had gotten in with his own key, tried to "hotwire" the ignition, failed, and left us with a nice van that won't run because of the cut ignition wires!

Very fortunately, our things left in the van had not been touched, such as our sleeping bags and heater. We're really not sure why the fellow failed in his hot-wire attempt. Anyway, we removed the rest of our things to the hotel and this morning I took the keys to the local garage. They'll tow the van in sometime today and try to fix it Monday. They wouldn't even give me an estimate so I'd have something to worry about. Instead, they all looked sad and shook their heads as if it were going to take their entire crew of mechanics several days to fix it.

But I want you to know that the French police were really wonderful about the whole thing. I spoke to three of them about two hours after the discovery and about one block from the van. Well, they were sort of busy smoking while they talked about something I'm sure was vitally important. I have to admit that my French really wasn't all that bad, as they all understood what I was saying. As two of them drove off, one said to me, "That's too bad," and he really did look like he was very sorry. Well, then I turned around to speak to the remaining policeman but he had disappeared. The whole incident with the police was very comforting and reassuring. If I can't make is as a lawyer back in San Diego, at least I'll know that I can always return to Paris and live comfortably as a crook. I spoke with our hotel manager, who explained that when cars are broken into or stolen, you must go to the police station to report the incident. Supposedly, they never go to the car.

One side benefit: We now have our butane heater in our room and it really does wonders. No longer will we have to "go shopping" just to get warm. Gives you an idea just how cold this room can get. Last report it was between 33°F and 39°F degrees in Paris.

Being the really intelligent fellow that I am, I purchased a TV in the States that has an AM/FM radio on it. It features a plug that fits into any cigarette lighter, so I figured that it would be a lot of fun watching TV all over Europe. Well, after dragging it 8,000 miles, we discovered that there is a different system of lines on the European TVs, which probably explains why I can only get a short, unfocused white line. But, the radio works, so we've got it tuned to the local rock station. It plays anything, or I suppose I should say it plays everything. One selection may be Bach and the very next could be the Beatles. About 40 percent are American tunes we recognize.

March 27, 1975

10:35 p.m.
Paris

Debbie and I took the train to Chartres today to see the thirteenth century cathedral. It probably has the most beautiful collection of stained "rose" windows in the world. It was fun on the train as neither of us had to worry about the driving and we could enjoy the scenery. The cathedral remains as majestic and beautiful as I remember it from seven years ago. For lunch, we ate a couple of ham and cheese sandwiches Debbie had prepared in our room before we left. As it was cold, it was a very short picnic. Going "home" on the train, we met a retired Frenchman who seemed most eager to try his "Anglais" and let me try my poor French. He said he didn't like Paris very well because of the traffic and weather. He was most proud to say that he was from the wine country of Burgundy. When I asked him how long he had lived in Paris, he replied, "Fifty years!"

A few nights ago we went by Victor Hugo's house, which was quite interesting. Turns out, he was something of an artist as well as a great writer. He must have been very fascinated with his name and initials, as several times he worked them into the scheme of the sketch. Also, enjoyed the Museum Carnavalet, which has several models of what Paris looked like during the fifteenth century.

I was just reminded by Debbie that I forgot to mention our excursion to Sacre-Coeur, which was pretty unforgettable. The reason we climbed about 300 stone steps that wound around forever in the dark to the top: From there we could look out and see all of Paris. Trying to get down was amazing, as you get down the same way you got up. There's barely room enough for one person to get through, let alone two people going different directions. We met a little English fellow on the way up who told me he was "terrified." We helped him past us, as I'm sure the others coming down also did. He's probably still up there, too afraid to come down. Anyway, if you are coming over to Paris, I suggest you avoid the climb to the top of Sacre-Coeur, unless you're a little crazy. If you are, you will probably have a ball—you'll certainly have companionship.

April 4, 1975

9:30 p.m.
Paris

Well, we just survived the second of two "tours" that stayed in our hotel. Both were high school groups, at least physically. Mentally, they all belonged in front of TVs watching Sesame Street. Of the two groups, Canadian and American, the Americans were by far the ruder and the noisier. My earlier judgment about the Japanese was probably wrong—they have a long way to go to catch up to us. I'm sure the kids were basically pretty decent kids; they probably hadn't much experience traveling in hotels or, for that matter, being in Europe.

Yesterday about 9:00 a.m., someone tried to open our door. When I asked what was going on, the person went down the first flight of stairs. We figured the fellow had just forgotten what floor he was on—even I did that once. However, about a half an hour later we learned that the Indian doctor who was staying below us had a $1,000 camera taken while he was out eating breakfast. Naturally, we're both relieved that we were here at the time, as everything we had was in our room. I'm just about to tell Debbie that we will now take turns staying up watching the room. I'll give her the midnight 'til 8:00 a.m. shift.

A couple of days ago, we took a bus out to Château de Malmaison, about ten miles outside Paris. It was the home of Napoleon and Josephine, and the place he returned to following his defeat at Waterloo. The visit was a real hit with Debbie, as it was furnished with the furniture the couple owned at one time or another, and it was very easy to imagine them living there.

Yesterday, we went to the top of Notre Dame and got to go inside one of the two bell towers. It was absolutely amazing to me to see the wood used as supports, etc. on the inside of the tower. Debbie sort of frowned as she came out, probably because she didn't get to see the hunchback. I tried to tell her that the fellow is getting old and that he only rings the bells on alternate Sundays now.

Debbie meeting the gargoyles of Notre Dame, Paris, April 4. I'm the rather good-looking one on her right.

I must say a word about French pets, especially dogs and cats. They are the true owners of Paris, as they virtually control their owners. I thought Americans were nuts about pets until we came here. Most businesses have a pet that is pampered close to death. One of our favorite restaurants has three dogs. The coat taker at the Rodin Museum has a cat that she won't let anyone else even touch. It just sits all day long at the counter in front of her. The laundromat down the street has our favorite pet, a large goose named Oscar. You only have to watch a few minutes to know that Oscar is the real owner of the shop. The story could continue ad infinitum.

You are probably wondering where these pets go when they feel nature calling? Well, you only have to walk one block on any sidewalk in town to learn the answer. Since downtown living means very few backyards, all the "domestic" house pets head to the sidewalks, too. It doesn't take long to learn that you look at the different cathedrals and monuments only when you are standing still.

As we leave for Amsterdam in two days, I'd like to sum up just a little. Without a doubt, my two most favorite things in Paris were (a) seeing the impressionists' paintings in the Jeu de Paume and (b) eating in the Café Le Procope. Just asked Debbie hers—and she agrees with my two and adds number three, Malmaison.

What was the funniest thing? The guide at the Pantheon, who spoke only French and carried a recorded English message on tape. It was one of the worst tours we've been on. The guide did everything humanly possible to get a tip at the end of the tour. He wouldn't let us out until he put down the tape recorder and planted himself between us and the door with his hand out. Debbie and I just blasted out by him as I said, "Merci." You probably had to be there, but we laughed about him until we got back to the hotel.

Amsterdam

April 8–11, 1975

April 8, 1975

10:30 p.m.
Amsterdam

Before anything else, I must put in a note about something we saw in Paris the day before we left. It was one of the strangest things on Earth. Originally, in the Gallo-Roman days, the Catacombs were limestone quarries that later became a cemetery. Thousands upon thousands of bones are stacked neatly up against walls, with skulls by the hundreds placed in patterns throughout. It was unbelievable to see and comprehend that all of the bones were once actual people walking around living daily lives. One sign said something like, "Don't laugh at the world of the dead for you will soon be in that world." See what I mean? Eerie.

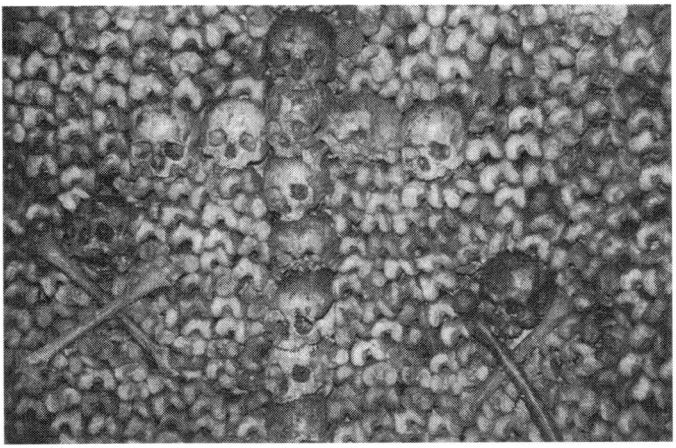

"Don't laugh at the world of the dead for you will soon be in that world."

The drive from Paris to Brussels went very well and we both enjoyed the scenery, especially the farms with the freshly born lambs.

Just outside Brussels, we stopped at a campsite called Huizingen and were happily surprised by the cost per night—a whopping seventy cents. Since we arrived at about 2:00 p.m., we decided to drive over to Waterloo (about eight miles away) to see the place where Wellington made Napoleon return to private life and his brandy. As we all know, Wellington went on to become a famous chef who was much acclaimed for his way with beef. Anyway, the battlefield looked like ordinary farmlands, and it was hard to believe that over 60,000 men died there in that battle. What did seem very real was paying about two dollars and fifty cents to see an absolutely terrible museum.

Camping was again extremely cold and rainy. We've decided to change from our original plan of going to Britain after Amsterdam. Instead, we'll head for Spain and hopefully better weather—at least warmer.

Yesterday, we drove into Brussels, which, driving wise, is sort of a miniature Paris. The Belgians have also added a small twist that the French haven't thought of, though: They hide all of their street signs on various buildings and use about one-inch lettering. Even if you know exactly where to look and have eyes like an eagle, you'll still be out of luck because the signs are much too dirty to actually read. But, somehow we made it and put the van into a VW garage for its 500-mile check-up.

As Brussels is not a great tourist attraction, we were able to see the sights in a two-hour walk around downtown. I think the most impressive thing to Debbie was when we saw a street repairman going to the bathroom in the street in front of a street full of shoppers. I really didn't think it was all that bad—after all, he did sort of face his truck.

Debbie bought lace for several of the relatives and a lace muffin holder for us. That night, we had a great spaghetti dinner and watched a little television—I never knew David Jansen was so fluent in French.

This morning, we took off to Amsterdam and again had a pleasant journey. Even driving through downtown Amsterdam went relatively smoothly, and it wasn't long before we had the van parked and found our hotel. Naturally, the hotel was 50 percent more than our *Europe on $10 a Day* said. After a huge hamburger at Wimpy's (I'm really kidding—it wasn't enough to keep a Mexican hairless well fed), we walked over to the red-light area, where the ladies of the evening sit behind picture windows and look out at their potential customers walking by. Debbie got a little upset when a couple of the "ladies" asked me if my name was Marshall. But there must be millions of fellows named Marshall that looked like me. They just made lucky guesses.

April 11, 1975

10:30 p.m.
Amsterdam

Not much to report other than we've had a really nice time in Amsterdam.

Surprisingly, the prices are higher than in Paris, but we've really enjoyed the stately homes overlooking the many quiet canals. The fact that all the buildings look like the seventeenth century adds a great deal of charm to the place.

As everyone must take English in school, we've had no problem at all communicating with the Dutch.

We especially enjoyed the Van Gogh Museum and our visit to Anne Frank's house. They've preserved the "secret Annex" very well so that you can see the movie star pictures Anne put up on her wall (now behind a sheet of glass) and the map on which Mr. Frank plotted the route of the advancing Allies. She died approximately two months before Holland was liberated. Stepping out of the house onto the quiet canal street, it seems impossible that such a tragedy could have ever occurred here.

This morning, we partook in the best brewery tour in the world—Heineken. Naturally, no one really cares about the actual tour. They're just waiting until the sample room at the end where they give you as much to drink as you like. In a little over an hour I put away five or six. I'm pretty sure Debbie was having a good time, too, until she learned that she was going to have to carry me back to the hotel. Somehow we made it and slept until about 3:00 p.m. Then it was a race to the aspirin bottle—then off to the post office, where we finally mailed off our ill-fated TV. Tonight, we are getting ready to leave Amsterdam for Lisse and then Arnhem, then points south, and hopefully the sun.

Don't ever volunteer to be the photographer after taking the Heineken Brewery tour.

France

April 14–18, 1975

April 14, 1975

10:00 a.m.
Avignon, France

Naturally, as we left Amsterdam, it began raining again; so although we were a little sad to leave the city, we were much less so because of the weather. Drove to Lisse, where Debbie went wild over the tulip fields at Keukenhof. We bought about fifty bulbs that will be sent to our parents sometime in September. From Lisse, we drove to Arnhem to see the Dutch Open Air Museum. But since it was raining, we went instead to the Kroller-Muller Museum just outside Otterloo. It had a great collection of Van Goghs, and we especially enjoyed his sunflowers.

We tried to find a place to stay around Arnhem, but the prices were really unbelievable. So we just kept going, crossed the German border, and stopped at a hotel in Siegburg just outside of Bonn. Big room, three beds, and toilet down the hall, for about ten dollars—however, no heat.

The next morning we were up at 7:00 a.m. and on the autobahn. In no time at all we were in Basel, Switzerland, where we had expected to stop for the night. Instead, promising ourselves we would return to Germany and Switzerland, we headed into France, stopping at Besancon. We stayed in an absolutely great campsite there. It was brand new and uncrowded, with all the facilities such as hot showers, clothes washing, etc. As it wasn't very cold, we passed our first pleasant night in the van. Rather, I had my first pleasant night—Debbie has come down with something between strep throat and the plague, which kept her up most of the night.

Next morning, we searched every town on the way to Avignon until we found an open drug store. She's a little better today, so hopefully the medicines are having some effect.

We're currently in a very large, crowded campground. We both had showers this morning, and a good egg breakfast, and we are about to walk across the bridge to Avignon. By the way, yesterday we drove into southern France and a sky loaded with sunshine. What a lift to our spirits! This morning, it's raining again.

April 16, 1975

9:00 p.m.
Narbonne, France

I forgot to tell you that I finally learned how to drive the van! After seeing the Kroller-Muller Museum in Otterloo, I decided to have my second lesson, since it's sort of in a secluded forest with very little traffic. Well, the kid has finally caught on and has stayed in the driver's seat about 80 percent of the time. Having driven through Lyon and Montpellier, I still marvel at the way Debbie was able to take us through Paris.

Avignon was fun to walk through, as it is a walled town and one gets the feeling of how something like it must have been during the Middle Ages. Never realized that seven popes reigned there, including two during the great "schism" days when there was more than one pope. Bought myself a small rod and reel on the way back to the campsite and immediately walked the hundred yards to the Rhone River, where I fished until dark. Of course I didn't catch any fish, but I did have some terrific bouts with some rocks and twigs. I returned with my lure and line intact, so all in all I count it a tremendous victory.

We drove to Arles and walked around the Roman arena and saw the baths. Those fellows were really amazing—they were everywhere, and everyplace they went they put up such tremendous monuments.

We're spending the night in Narbonne by the sea. It's sort of windy but very pleasant otherwise.

As we were eating this evening, Debbie and I talked about how much more we appreciate things now that we lack all the comforts. I don't suppose I ever really thought about how wonderful it is to have heat, or a really nice bed, a clean toilet, enough food, a bathroom with a shower right in your home, etc. Yet, I suppose that once back in "civilization," it won't be long before I start taking them for granted again. I hope not, though, as it seems so much more satisfying to actually notice how good a single roll of bread is, or how good it feels to sit in a bathtub. The wine here is probably no better than in California, but here we have taken the time to appreciate it and probably taste it for the first time. I suppose the less you have, the more you realize how good it is to be alive.

April 17, 1975

8:00 a.m.
Carcassonne, France

We spent most of yesterday morning trying to find a propane dealer so we could fill our stove cylinder. We finally found a dealer in Port la Nouvelle, which, if you check your best map of France, will show up as a dot about ten kilometers below Narbonne. However, once the cylinder was filled, we were on our way again and spent the later morning hours traveling to Carcassonne. When we arrived, we parked outside the huge castle and fortifications and had a leisurely lunch. After that, since we were both tired and since all the shops, stores, and museums would be closed until two, we put down the seat and slept for a couple of hours. Having your home with you at all times has certain advantages.

When we toured the fort, etc., we went through the museum and then walked along the ramparts. A great deal has been reconstructed so it looks pretty much just as it did originally—very impressive.

At our campsite later yesterday I went fishing, but the river won. It ate my lure and a lot of my line. But you wouldn't believe the size of the three I almost landed!

April 18, 1975

8:30 a.m.
Andorra

Andorra is an alcoholic's heaven. Everything is duty free, and so the main business here is selling name-brand items from diamonds to tape recorders. We bought a large bottle of Courvoisier for six dollars and fifty cents! We also splurged by getting a hotel room with a splendid view of the mountains and right next to the river that flows through town.

But Andorra is not that easily reached. If you come by car as we did, you'll encounter winding, steep roads that are sometimes wet from melting snow, hairpin turns, and so on. However, you'll see some of the most spectacular views as you're driving, which we thought made the trip worthwhile. On the way, we stopped for a picnic lunch and I took a couple pictures of Debbie fixing lunch (ham sandwiches and a little cheese and wine), with beautiful snow-covered mountains as a backdrop.

Debbie made a wonderful picnic on our way to Andorra.
We were the only people on the road.

Spain

April 20—June 3, 1975

April 20, 1975

10:00 p.m.
Barcelona

It was a pleasant drive into Spain, although we were getting a little tired of winding roads. Also, we (along with all the other cars) were stopped four times at the border and on the roads getting here by the *Guardia Civil*. One fellow made me get out and show him several things on the van. I suppose they're checking for illegal books, magazines, etc., as well as guns or narcotics. Anyway, it's beginning to get just a little annoying.

We walked all over Barcelona today and, since it was Sunday, we made a special point to be outside the old church in the gothic section of town about noon. The parishioners come out after services, a band strikes up a spicy Spanish tune, and several circles of dancing people just seem to appear. It seemed to me as if time stopped for awhile and that if something was happening in the outside world at that moment, it could never stop the music or the dance. They were really having fun; and although there were a few people taking pictures, you could tell from their smiling faces that they were dancing solely for their own enjoyment.

Then we went through Pueblo Español, which is a small village for tourists set up on the outskirts of the city. It contains replicas of representative buildings from each province in Spain. We bought a couple of tiles to use as hot plates and a very nice wooden cutting board.

Later in the afternoon, we went to a bullfight. Prices have certainly gone up in seven years. I sat in the same arena then for about fifty cents. Today it was three dollars and fifty cents per person for the cheapest seats in the sun at the highest level. Of the six bulls, two were pretty good and the fights were exciting. Naturally, we both hate the idea of such fine animals being destroyed, but it is not our country or custom. One matador was nearly gored; it looked like the bull hit him square as he was doing some fancy cape work on his knees. I was thinking at the time that if the bull swerved into him just a foot or so, he wouldn't have time to get up and out of the way—he didn't. The bull slammed him into the wall, and I think everyone in the place, including the matador, figured he'd had it. Yet somehow he wasn't gored, and he remained in to finish the fight.

One matador, Marismeno, seemed particularly skillful and killed his bulls in two attempts at the "final kill," or *estocada*. It was a little less agonizing to see the bull die quickly rather than see him suffer any longer. He was awarded two ears from his second bull and took a "victory lap" around the arena. The crowd loved him and threw flowers, coats, and several bags of wine toward him. He loved the crowd as well, and as his final salute, he picked up some dirt out of the ring and pretended to kiss it. Regardless of what anyone thinks of the morality of the killing of the bulls, no one can say it's dull.

April 21, 1975

9:00 p.m.
Barcelona

I forgot to mention that we're camped just out of town at Masnou, about a hundred yards from the beach. Yes, I went fishing today, and the ocean ate two of my lures. That makes Nature 3 and Hockett 0—but not for long.

We walked all over Barcelona again today. One special event was walking and climbing all over the church of the Sacred Family, which was left unfinished after its architect, Gaudi, was killed in 1926. It's just in the process now of being completed. The way the fellows were going at it, I figure it will be done in a hundred years or so. We especially enjoyed the naturalistic and free flowing style, rather than the heavy and rigid gothic style we're all so used to seeing. It's one of the best things in Barcelona to see.

Debbie still isn't 100 percent, but she's much better than before.

My Queen Isabella.

King Ferdinand fishing as he ponders the heavy burdens of his office.

April 24, 1975

11:00 p.m.
Cambrils, Spain

After a very early morning start on the twenty-second, we visited two monasteries—Montserrat and Poblet. Both were nice in their own ways, but I do think the numerous restaurants and commercialism surrounding Montserrat detract a great deal from it.

Later in the afternoon, we drove to Tarragona. Just before reaching the city, we stopped at the Roman aqueduct, which seems to be standing just as solidly as it ever did. We took a couple of pictures of it, and then I walked out on it about one-third of the way across. It's strange to actually touch something you've seen in pictures all your life. Anyway, I really enjoyed it.

Finally, we stopped at a little fishing village on the coast called Cambrils, where we've rested the last two days and picked up a little sun. I still have a perfect score with my fishing, but I do have a very nice lure collection now. The campsite was very nice—hot showers, etc.—which helped convince us to stay the extra day. I even washed the van after 2,222 miles and discovered it was bright yellow. I suppose I should wash it a little more frequently.

After lunch, we decided to take a walk around this beautiful little town. We came across several homes being built along the waterfront by gentlemen who apparently had never seen a woman before. They yelled and wolf-whistled for quite some time until we finally stopped. I looked at them, gave them my biggest smile, and yelled back, "Gracias! Gracias!" Needless to say, the natives were not pleased. Eventually, someone started to laugh. Shortly, everyone joined in, and I began working on my Nobel Prize speech.

April 26, 1975

9:45 p.m.
Benidorm, Spain

When we decided to stop at Benidorm, it looked like any other very small dot on the map. Since it's on the coast, we thought we would have a nice beach campsite like at Cambrils or Barcelona. However, upon arrival, we found a tourist city rivaling Miami Beach. Although we arrived over twenty-four hours ago, I could count the number of Spaniards I've seen on one hand. Most of the signs are in English or German. We both expected this sort of thing on the Costa del Sol and are a little disappointed to see it had gotten this far north.

On the drive here we stopped at Sagunto, which, if you know your history well, was the place the Second Punic War between Rome and Carthage began when Hannibal lay siege to the town. The ruins are magnificent and they've been pretty much unrestored, which is sort of fun. At least you know what you are seeing is the real thing, as opposed to the restoration done in the 1950s to attract more tourists.

As it's an out-of-the-way place, there were very few signs, and I'd bet no more than a handful of tourists visit the ruins in a week. Debbie and I happily crawled all over the ruins for about one-and-a-half hours. (I took a picture of her on the stage of the Roman amphitheater.) We found three small bits of pottery lying in the midst of the unrestored rubble, which I forgot to give the person at the gate.

I can't wait to get out of this place, so we will be pushing off tomorrow for Murcia.

April 29, 1975

9:30 p.m.
Granada, Spain

Sunny Spain has been a little wet the last couple of days—sometimes it came down so hard and in such "sheets" of water that I thought we were in the final scenes of *The African Queen*. I played the part of Katharine Hepburn and stayed in the van while I sent Debbie outside to do the dishes.

We're having a heck of a time trying to get our propane tank filled so that we can continue cooking. Gasoline stations don't carry it, so you are reduced to searching for refineries! We talked to a couple other people with "export" vans like ours who have had the same problem. Apparently, some have given up and purchased additional stoves that hook up to the bottle gas that you can get all over Europe. I'm afraid before too long we will have to do the same. That, added to the problem of having a 110-volt car in Europe, which is 220 volts; gets me a little mad at the Westfalia and Volkswagen people who didn't mention one word about either problem before we got here and who now seem utterly unable to help us out.

On a more pleasant topic, Granada is beautiful. Walked all over the Alhambra and Generalife and marveled at the intricate Moorish designs and architecture. Except for pictures, I've never seen anything like it. On the drive here, we passed a great number of houses that were cut into the side of the hills. The hill opposite the Alhambra, Sacromonte, is filled with them. Apparently, that particular hill is the gypsy domain.

Debbie's Spanish is amazing. It rivals my Russian or Chinese. But so far everything is going well. When you have money, everyone smiles at you and says "Buenos Dias" all the time. After lunch, I tipped the waiter thirty cents, and he was so happy I thought he was going to make me an honorary member of his immediate family.

May 2, 1975

10:00 p.m.
Malaga, Spain

As I write this, I can look out the front window of the van and see Malaga shining brightly about one and a half miles away, across a small bay. The van is approximately twenty-five yards from the beach with nothing obstructing the view from Malaga to Torremolinos.

We've spent a very pleasant and lazy two days here. Met a couple from Los Angeles, Nick and Monica, who have a van like ours and are traveling with their two children while he's on a teaching sabbatical. It was an enjoyable time, having drinks in their van and swapping stories and news about campsites.

Today we jumped on a convenient but smelly bus that took us to the heart of the town. Debbie bought some seven-dollar sandals that looked like they'd sell for about thirty-five dollars anyplace else. I know she likes them, as she told me she wanted to wear them to bed tonight. We also purchased a small rug for the back of the van, as well as a new knife, flower seeds, etc. The purchase of the day has to be my shoelaces that we looked all over town for. They looked great in the package and it said they were fifty cm long! Well, when we got back from town, we learned that we would probably have to stretch the laces to fit the shoes of a middle-sized mouse.

Van living continues to remain quite comfortable, now that we are used to it. Debbie's getting to be quite a little cook—we even had hot cakes yesterday morning.

Last month, we were over budget about $230, due to several factors such as our early hotel living and the long drive from Amsterdam.

Gasoline was our greatest expense, as it was about $207—however, we did travel about 2,500 miles! This month we are not going nearly as far and hopefully will do a little better.

May 4, 1975

8:00 p.m.
Estepona, Spain

We spent a relaxing day walking along the beach and reading Lash's *Eleanor and Franklin*. Debbie did half of the wash and a little shopping in the morning before our walk, so we're pretty shipshape now. Although it was a long way off, we could see the outline of the Rock of Gibraltar. Hopefully the weather will remain as clear and sunny as it was today so that when we camp in Tarifa tomorrow, we'll see a bit of Africa.

Yesterday, we took a trip to Ronda via some extremely winding roads. Although we enjoyed walking around the town and seeing the two bridges, we had a real scalping in the "touristy" restaurant by the "new bridge." I think the name was Don Miguel's. Anyway, after endless preparation among the waiters, one finally came up and gave us a menu and told us in English that the "menu of the day was very good." Well, we were in a little town in the middle of nowhere and we've had several great meals in Spain so far, so we decided to trust him and get the "menu of the day." We nearly fell over when he brought out alphabet soup! Next, a little macaroni, and finally two thin pieces of ham such as you'd put on a sandwich. A real Spanish meal.

We did a little shopping; Debbie picked up some tennis shoes, while I got some leather sandals.

Next, we took a pleasant twelve-mile drive out to the Pileta Caves. The last three miles were over an unsurfaced road so it seemed like a real adventure. After finally arriving, we stopped and parked our van and climbed an additional 150 yards by rock steps to the entrance of the caves.

We arrived just in time to go on a tour with a group of Spanish schoolchildren who were apparently on some sort of field trip. The caves were discovered by our guide's grandfather in 1905 and are filled with drawings by prehistoric people as far back as 25,000 years ago. Also, there was a pile of pottery that supposedly were the oldest such remains in Europe.

The caves themselves were a lot of fun to see; they had obviously not been commercialized, as were the Nerja Caves we saw just before Malaga. Rather, you have to step around great puddles of water and mud. Very few guardrails, and the guide lets you wander pretty much where you want to go. We spent quite a bit of time looking at the charcoal drawings on the walls. Several were of horses, fish, and antelope, but also there seemed to be a great deal of "Neolithic Shorthand" . . . a series of lines and slashes that obviously meant something to them, for the caves were filled with it. They looked a little something like this: mmm E <<, etc., but not in any straight line as I have shown them. Instead, they seemed to be placed randomly about the cave, some being placed on top of others.

Debbie was so fascinated with the drawings that she slipped on one of the muddy sloping cave sides. As she fell, she grabbed one of the rope railings, which came down with her, along with the seventy-five-pound concrete block it was attached to. The block hit her in the back, and she has about a two-inch laceration, which seems to be mending nicely. Fortunately it wasn't a deep cut, so no stitches were necessary. Debbie took the whole incident like a champ and still enjoyed the caves.

One small amusing thing about the tour: Apparently, there is no admission price, so when the tour ends at the entrance of the caves, you discover that you're locked in! When you turn around, you find the guide setting out his array of postcards, beers, cakes, etc.! Well, I planned on tipping anyway, but to get out I bought a postcard for a dollar and twenty cents. The guide was very happy to let us out after that. But, I really can't blame him. A fellow's got to eat, and nobody seems to be giving food away.

The Banana—If it gets better than this, I want to be there!

May 7, 1975

9:30 p.m.
Sevilla, Spain

After camping at Estepona, we drove down to the southern tip of Spain and camped at a beautiful site at Tarifa overlooking the Straits of Gibraltar. All afternoon huge ships, mostly oil tankers, passed in front of us. We could see the outline of Africa easily just by glancing out our window. That night we could see Tangiers sparkling brightly.

Another notable thing occurred at Tarifa: The "Big Banana," as we have nicknamed our van, received its first good-sized dent. While backing into one of the camping lots with Debbie looking out the right-hand window to guide me, we hit a two-and-a-half-foot stone well that I didn't see. You might be asking why Debbie didn't warn me about the well since she was the "lookout" and did see it. Well, I asked her the same thing, although I must admit I may have put my question to her a bit heatedly. She responded that she felt the well was so big, anyone could have seen it. Anyway, it's all fine now, but have you ever tried to sleep in separate bedrooms in a van?

I just happened to think of another small item that crops up from time to time: new clothes. Now, really, Debbie isn't dressed in rags like we see on some of the poor people. Her rags are so much cleaner. Anyway, despite my best efforts at frugality, we now have a clothing allowance for the year, so Debbie spends a good part of each day looking for the nearest I. Magnin. Don't you think fifty dollars is a bit high for a clothing budget? After all, a year really isn't that long.

May 7, 1975

In Sevilla today we toured Isabella and Ferdinand's palace, as well as the Giralda, a museum minaret that was converted into a bell tower after the reconquest.

We had a five-dollar lunch in town—actually, what I ordered wasn't all that hot, but Debbie graciously offered to switch plates with me. I just knew keeping her around after the car accident would pay off sometime! After lunch we walked to the huge cathedral but were told by a fellow who walked up to us that it was closed for the siesta 'til 4:00 p.m. Seemed like a nice sort of chap, for he told us he knew about a lace "factory" close by that was still open. Then, he offered to show us where it was! Can you believe how far they will go out of their way to be nice to strangers? Well, when we got to the "factory," he knocked on the door and someone unlocked it for him. Once inside, we were taken directly to a little room and shown everything from lace to leather jackets for about a half hour. Our friend even did the showing, and somehow he knew the prices of every item. I asked him where all the factory workers were, and he said about thirty miles away! Debbie asked him about coming down on some of the prices—well, he looked up incredulously and said that they were already "factory" prices. Since we did see a beautiful lace table cover for about eleven dollars, we decided to get it. Do you suppose our friend got some sort of cut?

Along with the lace, Debbie and I both got a small dose of "Montezuma's Revenge" by drinking some of the water (we think). Debbie's asleep right now trying to shake it off.

May 12, 1975

10:00 p.m.
Toledo, Spain

Before hitting Toledo, we stopped at Cordoba for a couple of days, one of which was extremely rainy. We enjoyed its unusual mosque and cathedral (as the cathedral is built within the mosque).

Outside Sevilla we tromped all over a Roman city called Italica, which is in the process of being restored. Both of us remain quite amazed at the Romans, in that they appeared to be everywhere and left such tremendous monuments.

Driving to Toledo we saw a couple of castles, which we got out and explored. The one at Consuegra was the best preserved castle-fort I've ever seen, though it hadn't been restored. We spent a couple of hours climbing over walls and through the various rooms, trying to figure out what they were.

Arriving in Toledo, we met Mike and Edith, a very nice couple we had met camping in Granada. They have the same color and type of van we have, so they have been most helpful in hints about the maintenance of the car. We went as a foursome into Toledo and had a great time walking around. We all ate lunch at a small restaurant they discovered and had chicken salad with tomatoes, egg and squid, and bread and wine for ten dollars for all of us.

I bought a nifty German electric shaver for twenty-two dollars, as I somehow managed to lose the cord on my shaver. As it can work on either current, it should be useful back in the States also.

By the campsite, I went fishing in a stream loaded with carp—that's right, not a bite. I'm even using the bait that two Spanish kids told me was foolproof—boiled potato. Anyway, I'll give it a try tomorrow.

May 17, 1975

1:00 p.m.
Madrid, Spain

Although there is absolutely nothing that we "have" to do, it seems like we're always doing something. I've been meaning to write in this log for the past two days, but just never had the time.

We arrived in Madrid after the short drive from Toledo and were quickly engulfed by the traffic. Although Madrid's traffic is not quite as bad as what we found in Paris, neither of us is crazy about venturing out in it again. After getting lost a couple of times, we found the American Express and happily received nine letters. As we hadn't received any mail in about forty days, it felt a little like Christmas. After getting lost only a couple more times, we found the campground where we hope to remain for a couple of weeks.

To get to town, we must first take a bus ride that's pretty unbelievable. People are jammed onto this bus as if it's the last one for a month. The bus itself has to be a gypsy reject, as it has no shock absorbers and you are literally jolted into town. If you survive the trip, you then get off at the last stop and get on the subway, which is probably a shade less hazardous than the bus trip.

May 21, 1975

11:00 p.m.
Madrid, Spain

Four days ago, I was in the middle of explaining how we seem to be continually doing something when I was called to a spaghetti dinner with our neighbors Mike and Edith. The following day we spent a rain-soaked late afternoon at the bullfights. A couple shopping trips, another dinner, and a visit to the Air Force base just outside of Madrid to help fix another friend's dented bumper, etc., have quickly brought us to today. Time is going by at a tremendous rate, yet we have never been happier. The people we continually meet on the road appear happy and full of vitality. We haven't seen a great deal of Americans traveling about Europe—they still remain the exception—but we do see a great many Australians and other Europeans. The Japanese are only in the bigger cities and are almost always on a very large guided tour.

After all we've heard about the Prado, neither Debbie nor I were very thrilled by it. I suppose the Jeu de Paume in Paris spoiled us, as we much preferred the French impressionist painters to El Greco, Velazquez, and Goya.

I've enjoyed food shopping here, which is something I couldn't stand to do back in the States. Here you can select the fish you want, and the butcher will clean and fillet it in a matter of seconds. Because of the great variety of meats, fish, etc., it's fun simply to wander around the different stalls. We're still not used to the siesta from 2:00 p.m. to 4:00 p.m., when everything shuts down. However, our dinner hour is now about 8:30 p.m., which is somewhat close to the usual Spanish dining hour of 9:00 p.m. We've enjoyed trying some of the local dishes such as paella—a sort of rice, seafood, chicken, beef, and black-mussel combination—as well as the wines and *cervezas*. Although we've been out for two and a half months, I really don't feel like a bum, as I once thought I might. In fact, before the trip I sometimes thought I might get bored, or at least feel that I ought to be working. Thus far I'm happy to say that I've had no such thoughts—right now, I feel like I could do this same thing for years and not regret it.

May 29, 1975

10:00 p.m.
Madrid, Spain

Tomorrow we leave Madrid. We've had a very pleasant time here, but it's time to move on. Seeing a lot of Madrid with Mike and Edie helped make this city even more enjoyable. Mike is a self-confessed bootlegger who was, as he puts it, "put out of business by Roosevelt," who helped repeal prohibition. He's worked as an Air Force photographer for many years and was the "sound" man on the Bob Hope Christmas tours for eighteen years, so he had lots of stories to tell.

His wife Edie is extremely nice and just as interesting. Originally a German, she grew up during WWII in Berlin and told us of the bombings and Russian occupation immediately following the end of the war. It was very much like listening to a character out of Leon Uris' book, *Armageddon*.

The four of us spent a very late evening at a local flamenco nightclub a couple of nights ago. As Edie had made reservations, we had a great table that was right in front and actually touched the stage. It could have been my imagination, but the dancing just didn't seem very "spontaneous" or gay. Rather, it appeared like the dancers were just going through the usual routines. I checked the menu to see if perhaps we might have gotten into one of the tourist traps, but discovered we were safe, as the menu was only in French and English—everyone knows the only people traveling in Europe today are the Japanese.

A couple days later we went to a festival in one of the large parks, where livestock, wine, food, and crafts from all of Spain's provinces are displayed yearly. Debbie and I especially enjoyed the chorizo—a sort of barbequed sausage that we had with local wine.

We dropped by the Royal Tapestry factory and saw how they made and restored both tapestries and rugs. The pretty guide told us that it takes approximately ten years to become a master. As there was absolutely no sales pitch—who could afford a $20,000 tapestry anyway?—we were very pleased with the tour and learned a lot.

I bought a plastic ten-litre (two and a half-gallon) container, which we filled at a local bodega with the local vino. As we go through about one litre a day, it will really cut down on our having to lug around one-litre glass bottles.

I can't close this section on Madrid without a couple words about the "mother and son" team who started camping in the space next to ours about a week ago. Although they are Americans, they've been in this campground for the last five years! They were originally living in a large, rented trailer. However, the rent was raised and they decided to move out of the trailer and "tent." But the "tent" was an old, leaky collection of shredded material that had to have been passed down from the Civil War and was just barely able to cover her body, along with her twenty-five-year-old son's. All of their "things" were placed on the camp wall without protection from ants, rain, etc. In front of the tent, they arranged two or three of the world's rattiest looking chairs, including the front seat of a car. I took a picture of the scene, but, even so, I don't think anyone will believe it. How did they earn their money? I have no idea, but we never saw either of them go off to town regularly. I'd write more about them but won't, as children someday might get a hold of this. They were a real "attraction," as all the other campers would come by and pause to stare in amazement.

Our neighbors in Madrid.

May 30, 1975

11:00 p.m.
Aranda de Duero, Spain

We woke up very early and got a good start on the day. By ten o'clock we were at the monastery—the palace of Philip II at El Escorial, which he had built after defeating the French in some battle in Flanders. The crypt, which contains most of Spain's kings and queens, was probably the most spectacular thing about the place. Perhaps the most interesting thing otherwise was that Philip II had his bedroom just off the side of the church's altar so he could still see the services when he was too old and sick to walk. We took an early tour, which we thought was pretty crowded until we saw a million people waiting to get in. One look at the line made us confirmed early-risers on days we want to see places.

Next we headed off over a brand new road (not even on our map) to Avila, where we toured the church and then the town by foot. Walked by the convent of St. Theresa, who was born in the town. We spotted two huge nests on the top of a bell tower that I guessed belonged to storks. Sure enough, later on our drive we saw a huge stork take flight out of a field as we drove past. Debbie wondered where the bundle with the baby was that they usually carry but seemed satisfied when I told her that the stork was probably just returning to the hospital.

Then we were off to Segovia for another walking tour around the old part of the town. Took two great pictures of Debbie by the Roman aqueduct (which apparently is still in use) and by a small fountain in a neat looking courtyard. Off again, we headed north until we hit Aranda de Duero and lots of rain.

Debbie at the Roman aqueduct in Segovia.

June 1, 1975

5:00 p.m.
Santander, Spain

We woke up yesterday morning to the clap of thunder and the beginning of a tremendous rainstorm that lasted several hours. We headed north again through spotted patches of rain until Burgos, where we stopped at a *supermercado* to fill up on two days of food, since the next day was Sunday and nothing would be open then. It was the usual open market with hundreds of people shopping at various stands. We saw several people selling live rabbits, which bothered us a little as we usually think of a live rabbit as a pet. Another unusual sight was a stack of six cartons of snails. Now a snail as food doesn't seem unusual, but a great number of these had decided to make a run for it and were getting out of the boxes and onto the floor like crazy.

Then we continued north, until we stopped at the caves at Altamira and took a tour with a group of Catholic girls. Although there were several nuns, the girls acted as if it was their first day out of reform school, as they continually left the walkways and tried to break off pieces of stalactites as souvenirs in front of everyone. The paintings themselves were worth seeing; they are remarkably well preserved and look as if they could have been painted yesterday rather than 15,000 years ago. Filling the ceiling of one cave were pictures of bison, reindeer, etc., and the average size was about five feet in length. One picture the guide said was interesting because it was very similar to an American buffalo.

June 1, 1975

On arriving in Santander, we were greeted with more rain. It continued all night and morning and, in fact, just let up about two hours ago.

June 3, 1975

10:30 p.m.
Pamplona, Spain

Most of the drive from Santander to here was quite beautiful except for a huge stretch through Bilbao, which has the worst smog I have ever seen. Hundreds of smokestacks were emitting smoke unchecked, apparently Spain's industrial area. It was so bad, we saw a young girl walking on the street with a handkerchief over her nose and mouth!

Although I've never had hay fever, I seem to have acquired a severe case and am constantly sneezing and blowing my nose since Santander. We stopped at a pharmacy, but the pills haven't had any effect. Hopefully, it will cease when we drive out of here tomorrow.

Pamplona itself was a bit of a disappointment for us, as we expected to see a very large old city and instead found a bustling modern metropolis. It just couldn't have been this way when Hemingway wrote of the running of the bulls.

We walked through the "old town" and went to a very large *supermercado* and stocked up on food. We also went to the local post office and sent off a few postcards. I think we both felt that the "bull run" would be much better suited in Toledo, Avila, or Segovia than in Pamplona.

France

June 4–10, 1975

June 4, 1975

11:00 p.m.
Casteljaloux, France

For the second time, we crossed the Pyrenees Mountains, but found the pass to the north of Pamplona to be much easier going than the earlier route through Andorra.

We'd planned to spend the night in a top-rated campsite in a little town called Villeneuve de Marsan, but when we finally arrived and looked at it, the weeds were waist high, and the only bathroom was about two-hundred yards away from the campsite, attached to the bar just at the side of the highway. We were pretty tired from driving and were greatly relieved when we came across a municipal camping spot at Casteljaloux instead. The cost per night is quite reasonable—a dollar twenty-five or five French francs—plus it has all the free hot water you can use.

We met four South Africans here (Tom, Yves, Tilden, and another individual whose name I forgot) and have just returned from an evening of drinks with them. We talked a great deal about WWII, as they were all involved in it in various ways. Interestingly, they said that each became convinced that the war would be successfully decided in England's favor when Russia was attacked by Germany and thereby pulled into the war. I had thought they would say it was the entry of the U.S. into the war, or perhaps the successful D-Day landings.

June 5, 1975

10:00 p.m.
Perigueux, France

Except for my constant hay fever, we had a terrific day wandering about the Dordogne Valley, noted for its caves that were once inhabited by cavemen.

We first stopped to see the museum at Les Eyzies de-Tayac and were quite surprised at how developed their artwork was. I think the commonly held view that they were half men/half animals is incorrect, as the bone carvings of different animals were often quite intricate and well done.

While in the Dordogne Valley, we visited several early-man caves.

The art on the walls in a nearby cave, Font-de-Gaume, was excellent and every bit as good as its counterpart in Altamira. Debbie and I notice that the same method of painting was used in both places, in which the outline of the animal was first chipped out in the rock wall and then filled in, usually with dark paint. This probably means they communicated with other pockets of early men and traveled many hundreds of miles as far back as 30,000 years ago. Another similarity between the art was the way the surfaces of the cave walls were employed and incorporated into the drawings. Several bison had legs that were drawn on stalactites, and often small holes were employed as eyes, etc. It was all quite fascinating and definitely gave us the feeling that the people who produced such art were not nearly as primitive as we have been led to believe.

June 7, 1975

9:00 p.m.
Montreuil-Bellay, France

Hooray for France—I believe I've found a pill to stop my hay fever! I've been pretty miserable for the past week, but since trying the latest "wonder cure" this afternoon, I haven't sneezed once. If it continues to work, I'm going to erect a monument on this spot telling of the miracle—if I spread the story far enough, who knows, it may become the new Lourdes, especially since gas is so expensive and this is so much closer to Paris.

On the drive here we stopped at the Bisquit cognac distillery, which is in the little town of Rouillac. We wouldn't have even been on that road except that we got lost in Angouleme, took the wrong road out of town, and were in the process of taking several "back" country roads to get back in the main road on to Portiers. There is no way possible that many people visit the place, as they almost have to be lost to find it and it's not close to anything.

Anyway, as we walked to the reception desk I was getting just a little embarrassed for stopping as I was sure that they would think we were crazy. I made up a little story of how my attorney friend in Paris had suggested that we stop by their distillery and that was why we happened to be there. Well, they really couldn't do enough for us, as we were shown the entire plant by two ladies who spent well over an hour with us. When we left they gave us four small sample bottles of their cognac plus a couple of postcards. If I was embarrassed before, I was doubly embarrassed now because of their kindness. As one of the ladies was giving us the free sample bottles, a fellow who was obviously one of the bosses (or the boss) came up to us, and I said to everyone in the room that from then on their cognac was the only kind I would drink. Everyone beamed, especially our guides.

Upon our arrival here we got lost again, but eventually ran across a small out-of-the-way wine-tasting place run by a little old fellow. He also went to great extremes to be nice to us and let us try several of his wines out in his "garage" and then took us into his private little bar for even more! We spent probably an hour there looking at his fossil collection and many antiques throughout the room. He took a couple pictures, which he seemed to enjoy immensely. He showed us his big guest book, which he was quite proud of, as he pointed out all of the things other people had written—very few in English. Anyway, I think he'll be pleased when someone translates what I put in his book: "We thought the wine was the best thing here until we got to know the fellow who took the time to show us his place." When I had finished writing, I looked around and he was writing a small note on the back of one of his personal wine labels. It read in French—"Your souvenir of your very kind visit to my caveau today—G. Nau." Then, I remembered that I still hadn't paid him for the ten litres of his best rosé, which we had earlier put in our plastic jug. He had forgotten, too!

Well, he had been so kind to us that I tried to give him an extra five francs, which he at first refused but with our persistence he finally accepted, but only after he had given us another bottle of wine with his personal label on it. As we said goodbye, he shook my hand profusely and then gave Debbie the "traditional" French kiss on the cheeks, which quite surprised her. Now neither Debbie nor I want to drink "his" bottles, as they mean something to us. I think we'll probably settle on keeping the bottle and using it as a candle holder.

M. Nau and I, in his caveau.

After Debbie complained that she still hadn't tasted enough wine, M. Nau allowed her to drink the entire barrel.

This morning we had tea with four English vacationers, all apparently retired. Everything was quite proper, with elegant serving sets (all matching), little cookies, and a choice of tea or coffee. Well,

June 7, 1975

after listening to our experience with Monsieur Nau, we gave them a little sip of our wine. Then they brought out their hard liquor. Two hours later (noon), Debbie and I were both so smashed we had to lie down in the car and never did eat lunch. They also were extremely kind to us and gave us seventy-five English tea bags, a camping guide of England, and nose drops for my hay fever.

When we went into the butcher's shop in town this afternoon for some lamb chops, the butcher started a conversation with us and before you could blink we were talking not only with him, but also with his wife and his pretty daughter who spoke a little English. We talked about everything from where we were going to what people did during WWII to the present day. All were extremely friendly, and we left with still another story of how kind people have been to us.

June 9, 1975

9:00 p.m.
St. Vaast-la-Hougue, France

This morning we got an early start and were walking the streets of Mont St. Michel by 9:30 a.m. As it is the third most popular attraction in France (Paris being first and Versailles being second), the small island fortress is a bit touristy. But as things had been restored so well, we really didn't mind so much. Also, as we had a great tour of the Abbey with an English guide, we felt that the trip here was well worth it. We wandered about the Abbey, the ramparts on the fortress walls, and the main street for about three hours.

We then took a leisurely drive to Cherbourg, stopping in Granville for a picnic lunch on a high cliff overlooking the ocean. The drive was a lot of fun, as Debbie read the various guides as we passed through each town to see what part it may have played in the D-Day invasion. We saw not even a trace of war damage anywhere. However, we did notice that the roads through the towns were much wider and better marked, as many of the towns had been completely rebuilt after the war. Several of the cathedrals had fairly new steeples or walls, etc.

I was surprised at how quickly we were able to travel up the peninsula to Cherbourg; it took just a few hours. I had always thought of it as being very large, especially since it took over a month for the Allies to capture the whole thing following the invasion. The land is truly beautiful, though—difficult to imagine thousands of people fighting and dying here. We're hoping to see the invasion beaches tomorrow.

I'm very happy to say that my hay fever is 95 percent cured by the French pills. However, now I can't seem to get over this craving for onion soup.

We're camped in a little place just north of the invasion beaches. As we are only two hundred yards from the beach ourselves, we took a walk there after dinner. We were there about ten minutes when the tide came rolling in over the vast plain. It came in at a walking pace and was one of the most unusual things I've ever seen. Water just flowed toward you as if it were a river. Within fifteen minutes, the vast plain-like area, which had earlier stretched out about a hundred-fifty meters, was completely covered.

June 10, 1975

9:00 p.m.
Bayuex, France

We stopped at Utah and Omaha beaches to visit the former's museum; it was inside a converted German bunker right on the beach. The beaches seem quite normal now, and only rarely can you see a rusting hull on the beach, at Omaha. Next, we drove to the nearby graveyard for American dead and walked through the nearly 10,000 crosses. We saw Brigadier General Theodore Roosevelt, Jr.'s grave, which has a cross just like all the others and is found between three privates and a first lieutenant. Almost all of the men had been killed during the landings or in the following few months. Not much you can say about a thing like this, except that we both felt terrible walking around and seeing how many young men gave up their lives so early. Debbie thought of how veterans' wives who saw this would see firsthand how lucky they and their husbands were. I thought of how well cared for the gravesites were and wondered what our gravesites in South Vietnam would be like in thirty-one years, now that the country has fallen to the North, which didn't look upon us as the "liberators."

Following that, we headed toward the port of Arromanches, where the Allies had built a tremendous artificial harbor to supply the invasion forces until the port at Cherbourg could be captured and then made ready for us. Surprisingly, a good deal of the artificial port is still there, although it had originally been designed to last only eighteen months.

After a very short drive to Bayeux, I bought some more French "miracle" pills and Debbie bought a set of lace coasters. Since we have been traveling a great deal lately, we pulled into this campsite fairly early to rest up for the rather long drive to Calais tomorrow.

Great Britain

June 11—July 5, 1975

June 11, 1975

9:00 p.m.
Dover, Great Britian

After the very long drive to Calais, we arrived just ten minutes prior to the ferry's departure. It couldn't have worked out better if we had planned it. However, I think we'll give that a try also next time. I thought the price was a bit steep for the twenty-one-mile crossing to Dover: eighty dollars and seventy-five cents for the van and the two of us.

The ferry was a Sea-Link model and quite modern. As it wasn't crowded at all, it was by far the most pleasant crossing of the seven I've made. We bought a couple bottles of Courvoisier for twenty-two dollars to ward off the cold British nights. The weather has been warm and sunny for the past week, so all in all, we both are in high spirits and extremely happy to be here.

June 22, 1975

9:00 p.m.
London

On our drive to London, we stopped at Canterbury to see its tremendous cathedral. After wandering about the tour for a little while, we were off to London—still more than a little strange to drive on the left-hand side of the road.

As we have been here for over a week, I have a lot of catching up to do. Primarily, we have been having loads of fun and doing as much in the way of entertainment as we can.

Thus far, we have seen four plays: *The Rocky Horror Picture Show*; *Harvey* with James Stewart; *John, Paul, George, Ringo, and Bert*, with Barbara Dixon doing the fantastic background vocals; and finally, *A Little Night Music* with Jean Simmons and Hermione Gingold. Although each has been very different from the rest, we have enjoyed them all a great deal. At the end of the plays, Debbie and I stage our own small dramatic role by trying to reach our bus stop across town before our bus leaves. So far, we have caught the last bus of the evening about six nights in a row, sometimes having to run the last several hundred yards and "beating" the bus by mere seconds. A time schedule is posted, but it is nowhere close to correct and everyone has told us to ignore it.

We spent two very pleasant evenings with Jean Gallo, an old high school friend now living in London. Like many Americans over here, she's working illegally in one of the many "tourist" shops by the major attractions. She took us to a pub last Thursday to see various amateur folk singers doing Irish ballads. The place was packed with young people who joined in on the chorus quite frequently.

Naturally, since there was quite a bit of drinking going on, it was a happy and loud group of people.

By chance, we ran into Mike and Nancy McCabe and have since gone as a foursome to all of the plays. Mike is a fellow San Diego attorney and old law school chum who just happened to be on vacation here with his wife. When we saw each other, we both nearly fell over from the surprise.

One day, as the four of us walked down Canterbury Street, Mike and I spotted a blue-striped three-piece suit that we both decided to buy. Once inside, Mike changed his mind and decided he liked a similar check suit and bought that instead. As the price was approximately ninety dollars, we both thought we were getting a pretty good deal. In fact, I plan on buying a couple more suits before we leave London.

One day Debbie and I went shopping for ourselves and bought eight beautiful Waterford Crystal glasses and a Wedgewood dish set with a flower design. We just simply couldn't pass them by, even though we knew we really couldn't afford them.

I also spotted a beautiful handmade Irish sweater that I bought for Debbie. It fit her perfectly when she tried it on, and I have little doubt that she'll be the envy of every girl in San Diego who sees it.

We've visited most of the outdoor sights as the weather has been beautiful. I think Debbie was impressed by the Crown Jewels in the Tower of London. Before that I used to be able to tell her there wasn't a diamond in the world big enough to express my love for her. She pointed at several and told me they would do nicely. Unfortunately, I was completely out of pocket change at the time.

While we were visiting the various museums in the Tower, a guard suddenly started blowing his whistle and ushering people out.

Apparently, someone had left a locked bag in the museum and, with the recent IRA bombings, there was a distinct possibility it was a bomb. On the way out, we noticed a marker on the floor saying that less than a year earlier a bomb had exploded on the very spot, killing one person and injuring several others. After that, the bomb scare seemed much more real to us. However, it fortunately turned out to be a false alarm.

We've seen something (or someone, rather) twice now who I never saw on my previous trip—Queen Elizabeth. Once, we just happened to be standing outside Buckingham Palace when she and Prince Phillip were driven by for a ceremony at Westminster Abbey. We next saw her riding horseback in a parade celebrating her "official" birthday. We were surprised at how old she appeared and that she never even smiled or waved at the crowd. I asked a little English woman about that, and she replied that the queen rarely smiled at such occasions.

July 2, 1975

9:00 p.m.
London

As we are planning to begin our tour of England, Scotland, and Wales tomorrow, I had better catch you up once again on our last week's activities in London.

One of the highlights was meeting the Nilssons, a delightful Swedish couple with two boys, who are traveling about Europe for three months. Surprisingly, except for a few trips to neighboring Denmark, this was their first trip out of Sweden. Their English was quite good considering the several years' interval since their schooling. As they are sort of new at traveling, they occasionally make a few blunders. One we saw was when they tried to get into The Bank of England to change some of their traveler's checks! (The Bank of England is the central bank of the United Kingdom. It is the equivalent of the United States Treasury Department. It sets banking rules, taxes, and financial policies for the UK.) They've invited us to visit them in Sweden sometime during our trip, and we are both eager to try and stop by toward the end of it, if possible.

We visited the Tate Museum and looked at the Hogarths and Turners. Although we liked these, we weren't very much taken with the collection of modern art there. Some of it really does look like the work of children.

We spent a great day and a half tramping through the immense British Museum, seeing everything from the Elgin Marbles to the special exhibit of Turner watercolors. Debbie paid particular attention to the Egyptian galleries and its mummies, while I got interested in a special exhibit about the Neolithic flint mining in

Great Britain. But even with all the time we spent there, we covered only a small fraction of the place. Perhaps the favorite room for both of us was the huge autograph gallery with signed letters, documents, etc., from various kings, queens, and other famous people. We saw a handwritten firsthand account of the execution of Mary, Queen of Scots, who required two strokes before her head was severed. I particularly enjoyed reading the last page of Charles "Chinese" Gordon's diary (written on the back of a telegraph form), which told his superiors in London that Khartoum would fall unless he got immediate reinforcements. As we know, the aid arrived too late and he died during the fall of the city. We were both surprised to see a long letter written by George Washington to a European friend, wherein he explained that America wanted no part of the present day (1799) European intrigues and merely wanted to "farm the richest land the world has ever known"—or something close to that. His handwriting was quite legible.

The last weekend, upon the invitation of the local postmaster, I watched a couple of local teams play cricket. My friend's team lost in a close game, but everything was forgotten in the little drinking session that followed.

Last night, we watched the replay of the Muhammad Ali/Joe Bugner championship fight, which Ali won easily. As Bugner is British, we were definitely in the minority. Bugner lasted a full fifteen rounds, but Ali's eight more years' experience made the difference. As the British announcer wound up the telecast, he commented that Bugner "is still the best white fighter in the world!" It shouldn't be too much longer before the British have themselves a very serious racial problem.

This afternoon, we went to a matinee of Neil Simon's new play, *The Sunshine Boys*—nothing special.

July 3, 1975

9:30 p.m.
Lincoln

We drove through Cambridge on our way to Grantham and caught glimpses of the university there. Once in Grantham, we stopped at my favorite eating establishment there, Hop Sing's Chinese restaurant. Seven years ago, Hop Sing had a little hole-in-the-wall restaurant with old wooden chairs and eight or ten tables. He also served the best food in town. Well, today his little restaurant is a lavish, two-story place with his own personal china pieces, etc. If anything, the food is even better. No place in the world makes sweet and sour pork as well as Hop Sing does. We were told that he has opened two other restaurants in nearby towns and is now quite the landowner in Grantham. Looks like the free enterprise system works pretty well if one is willing to work hard. Unfortunately, the British don't seem to have learned that, as they continually strike and wait for their North Sea oil to save them.

The pound has dropped ten cents in the last month. Everyone we meet tells us how disgusted they are with "the way things are going." Prices are skyrocketing while the British standard of living has been dropping for ten years. I expect the government will continue to cut back its spending and perhaps cancel some of its social programs rather than deal directly with the real causes of the problem. But enough of this.

Had a great time showing Debbie all of Harlexton Manor, the place where I stayed and studied seven years ago. It remains pretty much the same, although now it is being leased by the University of Evansville (Stanford having moved its campus to Cliveden). I must admit I felt a little strange walking around the huge, three-hundred-room manor house—in fact, I felt sad. I'm not altogether sure why I felt that way, but I think it was because I didn't "belong" there as I once used to. Anyway, it was nice to see the old place again.

July 5, 1975

8:30 p.m.
A little above Hexam

Yesterday, Debbie and I toured the huge cathedral in Lincoln, or at least the few parts that were still open to the public. Then we headed across the street to what's left of the Lincoln castle. Today it houses the criminal courts, but there is a place you can walk the ramparts along the defensive walls a little bit.

After a brief discussion, we decided we would drive to the city of York. I wasn't all that keyed to see York, but Debbie thought we ought to since my middle name is York and my mother swears that long ago our family sat around in that castle.

As it turned out, we're both glad we went, as we loved prowling around the old shops within the city walls. We climbed all over the old castle/fort from the days of William the Conqueror and then walked to their superb museum. Throughout the museum are mock-up streets of how York looked throughout its many periods. Walking through the huge cathedral, we went down two streets that had been in continuous use (for shops, etc.) for the past 1,900 years!

Leaving York, we drove a short distance before stopping at the side of the road for lunch (peanut butter and strawberry jelly sandwiches) and then taking off again to the area around Hadrian's Wall. We were surprised to see very little of the wall remaining, as all the travel posters we've seen show a fellow walking along a wall that stretches out for miles behind him. However, we did see the remains of a vast Roman town just outside Cambridge.

We plan on driving through Edinborough (Edinburgh, to the Scots) tomorrow, as the campsite here is terrible. The manager warned me they were having a "small problem" with the flies when we pulled in. Well, Debbie and I are now prisoners in our van. You probably won't believe this, but when we finally got to our campsite and I stopped the engine, so many flies were hitting our van that it sounded like it was raining! But, we figure we can live through anything for one night.

The Banana is running very well. She gets her 6,000-mile check-up in Edinburgh.

Scotland and Wales

July 8–30, 1975

July 8, 1975

11:30 a.m.
Edinburgh, Scotland

Today is a day of rest. I just finished reading Garson Kanin's *Tracy and Hepburn*, and Debbie is furiously reading the last two pages of Lash's *Eleanor and Franklin*. Debbie fixed us a delicious French toast breakfast this morning. After lunch, we plan on dropping by the pub across the road to listen to a couple of records we like. Additionally, I have to make a couple of calls regarding getting the Banana fixed, or rather checked.

Did you ever take a picture of someone and know instantly that you shouldn't have?

Yesterday, after dropping by the local VW dealer, we took the bus into town and walked all over. We just happened to be walking up the "Royal Mile" to the huge castle when we noticed that people were lining the streets. Well, we stopped to see what was going on, and twenty minutes later the queen, her mother, and Prince Philip were driven by in a beautiful old carriage. Apparently she is now in residence up in Scotland at Holyrood Palace (which means we can't see that this trip). This time she was smiling—the same with Prince Philip. Now some may accuse me of being a terrible cameraman, but I doubt that anyone in the whole crowd has a picture of the back of the threesome's royal heads when the carriage was ten yards past. I believe I may have waited a bit too long for the "perfect shot."

Then we fought the crowd to reach the beautiful castle that dominates the city. We had a little lunch there and afterward took our time prowling around the walls and building.

July 9, 1975

9:30 p.m.
Edinburgh

We're both pretty tired tonight. Early this morning, we took the Banana into the shop for her checkup and then we walked all over the city for the next nine hours until we could pick her up.

Once, while we were shopping on Prince Street, we saw people lining the streets again for another parade. Everyone there thought the queen was coming by, but it was the King of Sweden who apparently is here on a royal visit.

Later, we were walking on the Royal Mile and noticed people again lining up. Sure enough, the queen was to be rolling by again.

Well, we waited five minutes and sure enough, here came the family's black limousine. I got my camera ready to avenge my previous misfortune—and there rolled Prince Philip right into my sights. But where was the queen? A quick search, but to no avail, as she wasn't in the car. Another car? Nope, just looked. Then, I took the picture of Prince Philip. I got a dazzling shot of the back of his head as he is walking into a hallway—all only fifteen yards away! It's a shame *Life* magazine is out of business—I could have sold them the photo and made a fortune.

July 10, 1975

9:00 p.m.
Ballater, Scotland

Today was spent driving through beautiful scenery. Mainly, we saw huge valleys that had been slowly carved out by the glaciers thousands of years ago. We stopped at Balmoral Castle, which is really not a castle but a manor house the kings and queens of Great Britain have been using since Queen Victoria. It's begun raining, so we are not seeing Scotland at its best, but it's sure a lot better than what it could be.

Debbie's spending the evening reading while I'm writing several long-overdue letters to friends. One goes to Daver Atabey, an old friend living in Turkey who we hope to visit in late September or early October. I first met Daver in our senior year in high school. He was our foreign exchange student. It will be great to see him again.

Marshall's favorite picture of the trip.

July 11, 1975

10:00 p.m.
Lochness, Scotland

Today's drive was even more beautiful than yesterday's, if that's possible. On our way up to the small seaport of Nairn, we were on some fairly small roads that wound through farmlands and vast areas of grass dotted here and there by white sheep. Very peaceful. We felt like we were truly away.

We stopped at Nairn and bought two beautiful, handmade pottery vases (or bowls) that are different from anything I've ever seen. One has a design of flowers while the other has a cute representation of Noah's ark. Thus, we have broken our vows of not buying anything further that would put us over our budget. I think we are a lost cause. Anyway, the bowls are beautiful and very original.

We're staying at a beautiful campsite that faces Loch Ness. In fact, our car is only about thirty feet from the water and we have a great view of the lake. Naturally, we are ever watchful for "Nessie," the local nickname for the monster inhabiting the lake.

If you can believe this, two Canadians spotted Nessie yesterday about ten miles up from where we are. The camp manager said that she has never seen the monster, but sightings have been made here.

As it's been raining off and on for the last three to four days, our love for the Banana has increased tremendously. We feel like two bugs in a cozy house—warm and dry.

I plan on putting in some serious fishing time tomorrow while Debbie reads. This time I am going to catch one for sure—in a lake this size there has to be at least one stupid fish.

July 12, 1975

11:00 p.m.
Lochness, Scotland

There are no stupid fish in Loch Ness.

July 17, 1975

9:00 p.m.
Lake Windermere

Just finished listening to the first joint space project between the USSR and the U.S. on the radio in the van. Both countries' spaceships have now "docked" with each other, and the astronauts are now sharing a meal.

We've spent the last few days slowly coming down from Scotland. Most were uneventful as we just took in the scenery and enjoyed listening to the latest in rock music as we drove along.

However, yesterday in Carlisle proved to be one of the best days of our trip, as we stopped by to see Jack and Nora Pluckrose. We met them early in June at Montreuil-Bellay, France, and decided to take them up on their offer to drop by when we were in their neighborhood.

Jack and Nora took us up to Gretna Green, a small village just above the Scottish border that became famous for its "quickie marriages." Apparently there was no residency time required and the age requirements were much lower, so thousands of people eloped there and were married the "old" way by pounding an anvil with a hammer at the pronouncement of marriage. An act of parliament stopped any further marriages being legal around 1947, so now it's just a place for tourists to see.

Then we all had a "smashing" time playing croquet on their backyard lawn. All the pressure must have been on the other side as the Americans finished first and second in the first game. Debbie had some tough luck with the second game, and we finished at opposite ends.

After our second serving of tea, we went back to the campsite and dressed in our spiffiest clothes as we were then taken out to dinner in a very nice local inn. After we got a round of drinks, while we were still sitting in the lounge a waitress gave us each a menu and then returned a few minutes later to take the orders. Only when the first course was ready were we called into the other room where our table was. Both Debbie and I liked that arrangement very well, as we spent the waiting time in the comfortable lounge chairs.

The meal was the best I've ever had in Great Britain. I had salmon mousse with prawns, a steak, beans, potatoes, strawberry cake, and a great German Moselle wine. Debbie had something that looked a little like whipped up avocado and then veal Milanese as her main course. Then, it was back to Jack and Nora's house, where we all had a couple of drinks of Courvoisier, the only thing we were able to supply all day. As they have relatives in Los Angeles, we entreated them several times to visit Southern California so that we might be able to return their warm hospitality. I have a feeling someday they will come, and Debbie and I are already planning a list of places to take them.

This morning, we drove a little north to see the large section of Hadrian's wall near Carlisle that runs for several miles. Then, we went south and drove through much of the Lake District, which reminds us a great deal of the Scottish Highlands we just left.

Although there are many disadvantages in traveling about Europe in a van, we are very happy we chose to do so. You can stop and start whenever you want. Most important is the opportunity to meet new friends. If you are in a hotel, chances are you will never even meet your next-door neighbor.

I took a picture of Debbie enjoying a magic moment.

Would you like to see one of the most beautiful places on the planet?
Try Scotland.

July 18, 1975

9:30 p.m.
Rhyl, Wales

We woke up this morning to a light rain. As Jack told us a couple of days ago, "In Great Britain, if you can't see the mountains, it's raining; and if you can see them, it's about to rain." By the time we reached Windermere it had stopped, so we got out and slowly walked through town. There was a pleasant atmosphere about the village with little of the hustle and bustle we saw in nearby Keswick. Debbie even mentioned that she wouldn't mind having a little pottery shop in the village.

Then we headed down the motorway (M6) past Liverpool and took side roads to Chester. Although neither of us had heard much about Chester, we decided we'd stop to stretch our legs. It turned out to be a delightful walled city with hundreds of old-style shops to browse through. It reminded me a lot of York. The walls around the city have been carefully restored, so we took a quiet walk along the ramparts for about half a mile before we returned to the shopping area. Several streets had second-story shops that were all connected by walkways facing the streets. I've never seen anything quite like it before, and as the buildings were all restored, shopping around was fun for a change. Now Debbie, on the other hand, loves to shop anywhere at anytime for just about any length of time.

Tonight we're spending the night in a terrible campsite at Rhyl, on the northern coast of Wales. Again, Rhyl looks like a pleasant little dot on the map, but apparently it is the Welsh version of Coney Island, with hundreds of amusement parks and thousands of people. We are both looking forward to leaving tomorrow morning, as we know Wales has a lot more to offer than this.

July 20, 1975

9:30 p.m.
Chepstow, Wales

Yesterday it rained most of the day, so we satisfied ourselves with mainly just driving to Aberystwyth, where we spent the night. We passed through a lot of beautiful countryside and many quarries and slate mines. A couple of the mines were open to visitors and, but for the onslaught of rain, we would have gone in. As it was, however, since we didn't stop, Debbie and I started trying to guess as many different uses for slate as we could think of (which wasn't many) and about how it was mined. Anyway, when we get home, it will be something to look up and satisfy our curiosities.

This morning it was only slightly drizzling as we set off to Devil's Bridge, which is at the confluence of the rivers Mynach and Rheidol. According to local lore, eighth century monks commissioned the devil to build a bridge across the chasm. The payment for his service was to be the soul of the first to cross the bridge. The crafty monks then fooled the devil by sending a dog across first. Naturally, Debbie started feeling sorry for the poor dog until I lied and told her it was Pekinese—she hates Pekinese.

Anyway, the falls were beautiful, but we got a little damp as it began raining during our walk through the woods to the various viewpoints.

While looking for the campsite this afternoon, we got lost for quite some time in the town of Chepstow. For some reason, we kept going by this huge castle facing the local river. Well, on the third time by I decided to stop to see the thing and perhaps get some directions.

The castle turned out to be well preserved and contained several rooms, towers, etc., to walk around in. Believe it or not, we actually found ye old bathroom connected to the soldiers' quarters. Yep, it was about an eight-by-ten-foot room with a ledge of about one foot on the southern wall. As we approached the edge, we could see that it consisted of two iron bars upon which one could sit and make deliveries to the river, about 100 feet below! Apparently it was the only room built in part over the river. Very clever of those early Britishers, and it cut out all those plumbing repair bills, etc.

As we spent quite a while wandering about the castle, we decided to go the whole route and splurge by buying a thirty-five-cent guidebook. Turned out this castle was almost always in the hands of "chickens." The owners of this huge, massive castle probably surrendered more than any other castle in the world. Several times when they had people in the castle wanted by armies outside that were prepared to fight, the fugitives were given over immediately. It really shook me up—sort of like finding out about the Easter Bunny.

Just finished my seventeenth book of the trip—*The Beria Papers* by Alan Williams. Nothing special.

July 21, 1975

6:00 p.m.
Bath, England

After a short drive to Bath, we finally found a parking place and set out to see the city. As it was once the place where the Romans took their holidays in Great Britain so they could relax in the warm mineral waters, we naturally headed first for the site of what's left of the Roman baths. The place was jammed with tourists, but we managed to see the museum and walk around the warm water still in existence. We also both drank a glass of water from the "pump" next to our room. Apparently, in the seventeenth century people came from all over to drink the water, which they thought was very healthful. It tasted exactly like warm water with perhaps a slight trace of sulfur.

We also stopped at the cathedral to see its famous fan-vaulting ceiling. It's really quite amazing to see, as it transforms this huge stone building into a light, airy cathedral, making it seem much more comfortable inside.

We're parked in an extremely nice campsite—our refrigerator is filled with food—the skies are deep blue—so we're really living well today.

July 22, 1975

10:00 p.m.
South Molton

After we both had hot showers and a little breakfast, we headed in the direction of Wells. Just before the town we took a small detour to see Wookey Hole. We didn't know anything about it before we got there but, as we had the time, we thought we'd give it a try.

Wookey Hole turned out to be a vast complex of interesting rock chambers connected by an underground river. Just this year a tunnel was dug that allows visitors to see nine of the chambers. Scuba-diving archaeologists have followed the river back through eleven other chambers and are currently trying to establish the source of the river.

The guide had quite the tale to tell about the Witch of Wookey Hole. Apparently an old woman goat herder used to live in the cave about 400 AD (just about when the Romans left Great Britain), and the local superstitious fold thought she was a witch. They petitioned a local church to do something about the situation, and a local priest was sent in with holy water to exorcise the cave. It's thought now that the priest found her dead in the cave and buried her, then returned to the people outside and told them that when holy water hit the old woman, it turned her to stone. The people believed it for hundreds of years. Inside there is a stalagmite that looks a little like a woman (I think *very* little).

Apparently modern archeologists thought the story was just a wild legend until a couple years ago, when they uncovered the bones of an old woman who was clutching a small "crystal" ball made out of stalactite! Buried with her were two goats that had apparently been tethered next to her but died of starvation after the woman died.

The guide told us that her remains were exhibited in the Wells Museum, so being that we were so fascinated by the story, we went to see her. Sure enough, her bones were mounted on one wall and on the case beside them was a marble-colored ball about the size of a hardball.

Wells itself is a neat little village to walk through, which we did after the museum, so we were very happy we stopped.

Next stop was the ruined Abbey at Glastonbury, which I wished we had avoided—it consisted merely of the foundations and a couple walls of an old cathedral. We've seen almost too many cathedrals by now, and foundations of them are just a bit too much. It did have a small grave with a sign that said King Arthur had been buried there until he was removed in the sixteenth century. Nope, the sign didn't bother to say where or why.

July 30, 1975

10:00 p.m.
London

Well, we're about to leave London! On the way here, we stopped at Land's End at the very tip on Cornwall, Penzance (no pirates now) and Stonehenge. We enjoyed Stonehenge a great deal, although it looks exactly like its pictures. The surprising thing for me was the tremendous size of the stone blocks—none of the pictures I've seen have ever done that justice.

Debbie decided that she wanted some additional Wedgwood pieces, so we completed our set (I hope).

We noticed that Neil Simon's "smash hit" of the "Sunshine Boys" had quietly closed during our trip and in its place was Henry Fonda's one-man show of "Clarence Darrow." Fonda was super—both of us loved the show.

One afternoon, a family from Los Angeles parked next to us. We were all surprised to see that there was only one number's difference in our license plates. That led us to discovering that we picked up our cars on the same day, five months earlier! We nearly fell over when we learned we had also been on the same flight from Los Angeles!

We spent one very pleasant evening in the King's Head Tavern just a little down the road from our campsite at Chigwell. The pub was apparently mentioned in the Charles Dickens's *Barnaby Ridge* and is still quite a popular spot. We went there with a naturalized Hungarian couple on vacation from military duty in Germany. While we were there, we saw many members of the cricket team I had watched earlier. They've kept their perfect record of losses intact and took a lot of kidding during the evening. All of them were quite curious about the U.S. and very disgusted with the way things are going in Britain.

We spent a day at the home of Hussein and Gretchen Abbo yesterday. Hussein is an artist in London who has done everything from designing cutlery for the King of Morocco to designing furniture ads for the newspaper. The man has a great sense of humor, and it seemed like we were laughing all day. They hope to move to San Francisco in the next year, so it looks like we'll have the chance to repay them for their hospitality.

Germany and Switzerland

August 5–15, 1975

August 5, 1975

10:00 p.m.
Baumholder, Germany

After crossing the channel to Ostend, we couldn't find a campsite and were forced to "free camp" at the side of the highway for the first time in our trip. We learned very quickly that having toilets handy is far more than a nice convenience.

The following day we headed for the military base in Baumholder to see our friends, Captain Jerry and Kathy Brown. We met them in Madrid and fell in love with their two children, Sherry and Becky. What a pleasure to be welcomed into a home after five months. I'm sure I'll never forget the huge bathtub here, the pancake breakfasts, etc. The children remembered us and were just as sweet as they'd been in Madrid. Debbie and I gave them a couple of dolls we purchased in Wales.

Jerry and I went to the Czechoslovakian border yesterday to see the base he and his men will be training in, a month from now. As he had seen a lot of action as a tank commander near the DMZ in South Vietnam, we traded stories of our respective professions all the way there and back.

Later, Jerry took Debbie and me out to the tank range in Baumholder, where we took a small ride in one of the tanks.

Jerry and his family will be transferred back to the States in about nine months, so we are already making plans to have them visit us in San Diego.

August 7, 1975

9:00 p.m.
Delemont, Switzerland

Yesterday, we dropped by Bad Bergzabern, Germany, to see Ilsa Krinksy. She's married to Dan, an attorney friend of mine in San Diego. Almost six months ago, we'd made plans to stop by and see them while they were here on vacation. Unfortunately, Dan was unable to get away from the office, and Ilsa came alone with the family.

This morning, we drove through Basel on our way here, changed a little money, found a campsite, and took a three-hour nap. Although we're taking things very easily, we just found ourselves exhausted this afternoon. It could be the weather—today was about the tenth day in a row it's been above ninety degrees! Everyone says the weather has been incredibly hot this summer.

August 10, 1975

10:00 p.m.
Geneva, Switzerland

From Delemont, we drove to Neuchatel and spent the night at a campsite just out of town and very close to the huge lake. Again, it was extremely hot.

Yesterday, we drove to Geneva by way of Vallorbe. At Vallorbe, we took a walk through a beautiful forest to the source of the Orbe River. I've decided that if I ever get ten million dollars, I'm going to buy that forest and stream—it was beautiful and perhaps the most peaceful setting we've come across.

When we finally reached Geneva, we learned that American Express (which hopefully is holding a lot of letters for us) had closed just twenty minutes before. That meant we had to find a campsite for a couple of days (since AE doesn't open on Sundays). After searching to no avail for the first-class campsite listed in our book, we learned at a gas station that it had closed. So, it was back across Geneva again to our last hope of a campsite. We must have gotten one of the last sites because this place is packed—but it's full of good facilities, it's kept clean, and we're right on the lake. I went swimming for quite awhile this afternoon with my mask but never saw even one fish the whole time. Most of the bottom is sandy with a greenish moss in large patches.

Yesterday afternoon and this morning, a terrific lightning storm helped to cool us off. I must admit, we feel awfully smug sitting high and dry in the Banana when everyone else is getting soaked. There is no way in the world I could be a "real" camper.

August 11, 1975

9:00 p.m.
Zermatt, Switzerland

We received several letters this morning. One informed us of the death of a very close friend, Elizabeth Boyd. She and I have been close for about fourteen years—it's impossible for me to realize that such a vibrant woman is gone. I had just written her from Scotland, but apparently she died before it reached her. I cried when I read the letter. I even cried part of the way driving here. It just seems so totally wrong—she was only forty-eight. Fortunately, Debbie met her in February and saw firsthand the kind of woman she was. We shall miss her.

August 12, 1975

11:00 p.m.
Zermatt, Switzerland

If you've ever seen a postcard of the Matterhorn, then you've seen it as well as we have! The mountain has been entirely covered by clouds since we arrived—in fact, today it rained most of the day. We had tea with a couple of fellows who are going to try and climb it next week—nice guys, but I tend to think they are overestimating their abilities. This morning, we took a long hike into the hills around Zermatt and got soaked, and on the way back we stopped by the cemetery. It's filled with people who also may have overestimated their abilities. One girl was only twenty-five—she had fallen into a crevasse. Another was killed by "falling stones." Seeing that, we gained a healthy respect for the mountain.

The Matterhorn on a clear day!

August 13, 1975

9:00 p.m.
Lauterbrunnen

Woke up to a clear sky. So before we left we finally got to go see the Matterhorn. Naturally it looks exactly like the postcards, however, they couldn't show how powerfully it looms over Zermatt. It has to be the most impressive sight we've seen so far.

The drive here was beautiful. However, some of the roads in the passes were incredible. The Grimsel Pass just out of Gletsch, for example, had about fifteen hairpin turns as it slowly wound its way up one side of the mountain. The road had few guardrails, which added a special thrill all its own. Looking down from the top, the road looked a little like spaghetti.

The Lauterbrunnen Valley.

Lauterbrunnen is in the middle of a large, glacier-carved valley. It's loaded with waterfalls and would compare rather well with Yosemite. Just down the road, we visited the Trummelbach Falls, and they were tremendous. A rocky path leads you into the mountains for about fifty yards, where you can stand on various platforms and view the falls. The fellows who built the ledges and tunnels must have been scared out of their wits—one slip and they would have had a terrible day. Both Debbie and I were sort of overwhelmed by the force of the water as it pounds its way to the bottom.

August 15, 1975

9:00 p.m.
Lucerne, Switzerland

Having some problems with the Banana—her water pump won't work. Also, she's beginning to die a lot. Not sure if it's the altitude or what. We tried to find a VW place today, but everything was closed for Assumption Day.

Yesterday, we drove to Grindelwald and walked through the Gletscherschlucht, a path (sometimes tunnel) up a canyon beside a raging river. Again, you really get a feeling for the tremendous power of water and glaciers.

We walked all over Lucerne today, but fortunately all the shops were closed. Almost forgot to mention that we bought a beautiful handmade tablecloth in Grindelwald. No, I haven't forgotten that we also bought a lace one in Seville, but Debbie just seems to have this "thing" about buying anything in a shop window she likes.

Right now, we're sitting out another passing rain and lightning storm—dry and toasty. Chuckle, chuckle.

Just finished my twenty-first book—John le Carré's *A Small Town in Germany*.

Austria

August 19–30, 1975

August 19, 1975

9:00 p.m.
Innsbruck, Austria

Had the Banana in the shop today and got her lock and water pump fixed. Hopefully, we're all set for our trek south to Vienna.

We walked through the old section of town this afternoon. I bought Debbie a cute apron (something she had been after since Spain), and we stopped in a small ice cream place for a couple of banana splits.

The trip here was pretty uneventful, although we got a little scared as we almost ran out of gas in the rain going through Arlberg Pass. We just couldn't seem to find an open service station.

We did stop in Liechtenstein to mail a few cards home. We couldn't believe how small the place was, as it only took us about twenty to thirty minutes to travel the entire length of the country.

August 20, 1975

8:00 p.m.
Hallein, Austria

Today we conquered the Eisriesenwelt ice caves—although they came awfully close to doing to same to us. We are both so tired of walking and hiking that I'm sure we'll turn in just after I finish writing this.

After driving several hours to Werfen, we took a steep gravel road up the side of the mountain for about four miles. Then we hiked about one and a half miles to the tramway, which shot us up the mountain like gangbusters. It was a strange feeling, being in the tram; you know you're safe but you can't help thinking about what would happen if that little steel wire broke—and the sensation you get as you spring up out of the tramway station and watch the ground disappear below you is not something I'm going to forget for awhile.

Anyway, Debbie finally told me to open my eyes, and we were at the top of the tram. Then it was about a three-quarter-mile hike to a giant cave in the side of the mountain.

Then began the real hike—about 1,300 steps up through passages in the mountain that contain huge ice formations—some of which came from the last ice-age glaciers about 10,000 years ago. The guide "lit up" several formations by holding burning strips of magnesium behind them. Debbie spotted a man doing one of the stupidest things we've seen—he hacked off a piece of ice for a souvenir! We were glad to have seen the caves, though; if someone had told us how impressive they were, I don't think we would have believed it. It truly is something you have to see for yourself to believe. The first explorers must have just about gone crazy when they entered them for the first time.

August 21, 1975

9:00 p.m.
Salzburg, Austria

Tonight we're perched on a mountain overlooking the city of Salzburg, about three miles below and away from us. The sun is just setting now, and the lights are beginning to turn on here and there. The city is dominated by a huge castle on the hill in the middle of town, but from here it looks quite insignificant. I've got the van parked sideways, so it's as if we're in our living room looking out a picture window.

At the far end of the picture is the dark grey outline of another Alpine range. This one is sort of special, as it lies just across the border in West Germany and has on or near the top of it a famous place: the Eagle's Nest of Berchtesgaden, Hitler's mountaintop hideaway home.

This morning, we had a quick breakfast and headed for the tramway in Hallein, which took us quickly up the mountain to the salt mines of Durrnberg. The mines are huge—in fact, most of the time you're walking below the ground in West Germany! A couple of times the group entered lower mine shafts by way of unique slides, which small groups of about five straddle, and swoosh, they're off. Everyone is issued a white miner's outfit so as not to ruin anyone's clothes. Sound like fun? It was!

August 27, 1975

9:00 p.m.
Vienna, Austria

For several days, the weather has been terrible—rainy and cold. We spent a couple of them sitting in the van reading, etc., but finally when we were about to go stir crazy, we put on about two tons of clothes, jumped out, and braved the storm. We headed for the old part of town near St. Stephan's Church and just window shopped, and we saw some more Roman ruins under the old market-place. We had a funny experience in the pastry shop while trying a Viennese Sachertorte, as the waitress not only added a tip to her bill but also scooted back before I had put my change (about fifty cents) in my pocket and just slid it all into her purse. Both Deb and I were so flabbergasted that we didn't say anything. Anyway, the tortes, coffee and tea were about a dollar fifty and the tortes were about a dollar twenty-five.

We visited Vienna's art museum, the Kunsthistorisches Museum, but other than the Rubens paintings and statues, we weren't all that crazy over it. I guess we were really spoiled by the Jeu de Paume in Paris.

During all the rain, we read quite a bit of the history of the city, and naturally about the Habsburgs. We learned among other things that Beethoven was evicted many times because of his piano playing in the middle of the night; one of Maria Theresa's sixteen children was Marie Antoinette; Vienna was the spot where the invading Turks were finally stopped and driven away; well, I could go on and on like this for hours.

But, today was a beautiful, sunny day—so we happily dashed to the Schonbrunn Palace (the summer residence of Maria Theresa) to tour several of the rooms and the grounds.

In our tour, we noticed "Mrs. Olson" of the Folger's coffee commercials, and her husband, Fritz Feld. They were both very pleasant, and we talked with them for about half an hour. Fritz said he had been in 410 films! They had just returned from seeing Moscow and Leningrad and were in the middle of a two-month vacation.

"Mrs. Olson" and hubby Fritz Feld.

August 30, 1975

9:00 p.m.
Vienna, Austria

Tomorrow we leave Vienna for Graz, Austria, before crossing into Yugoslavia. We had a great time here, despite several days of rain. We've eaten a couple of good meals out—once in a Greek place, where we stuffed ourselves on the "Hellas" plate, and also at the Wiener Rathauskeller, a large decorated hall under one of the major buildings on the main circle. We both had wiener schnitzels, salads, beer, and strudel.

Although many Austrians have been very kind to us, it seems like the majority tend to be a pushy lot; rather than line up and wait in turn, they just barge on to the trams *en masse*.

Although we have been planning for quite some time to fly to Egypt for a few days, we've just begun thinking about also visiting Israel. So, I've been checking our finances, maps, etc., to see if we'll be able to arrange it. Looks like a fifty-fifty chance at the moment.

Yugoslavia

September 3–7, 1975

September 3, 1975

9:00 a.m.
Rijeka, Yugoslavia

Crossing into Yugoslavia was a breeze—the visas cost us nothing, no one searched our car, and we purchased gas coupons so that we'll pay less than anywhere else is Europe, about a dollar twenty-three per gallon.

On our way to Ljubljana, we stopped in a couple of "supermarkets" and quickly noticed the lack of variety among the goods. From the outside, one store looked huge, but on the inside I noticed one complete aisle filled solely with sugar!

Camping in Ljubljana, we met Captain John Lauder; his wife, Betty; and his daughter, Alexis. He's about to return to Northern Ireland for a second tour of duty. He too feels the situation there is senseless. We split a bottle of Yugoslav wine with them and fell in love with their dog, Angus. They mentioned news we hadn't heard—that two weeks ago some Americans snapped an underwater picture of the Loch Ness Monster.

Yesterday, on our drive here, we stopped to see the caves in Postojna. They are especially nice since you get to ride a small train for one and a half miles into them before you walk through the main chambers. We were told that the caves are about fourteen miles long. The caverns we saw were quite beautiful, being filled with stalactites, etc. The only living inhabitants are blind, flesh-colored salamanders that live off the plankton in the water. We saw a few, about the size of your middle finger.

We camped twenty yards off the Adriatic at a campsite just outside of Rijeka. Most of our fellow campers are from West Germany, or countries behind the "Iron Curtain." It's a beautiful spot, and yesterday I took my goggles and did a little swimming. Last night, Debbie and I sat on the rocks nearby and watched the lights come on in the village across the water. Thus far, Yugoslavia has been very kind to us.

September 7, 1975

3:00 p.m.
Split, Yugoslavia

It seems as if the people are friendlier as we head south. Quite often now we see the traditional black dresses and scarves, and we often see horses, carts, donkeys, etc. off the main road between towns. But existing right along with these people are the modern-dressed town people, who look very much like people from any other country.

We've run into several good stores in large towns that are quite comparable to those in the U.S.—there just aren't nearly as many.

A couple of days ago, we met two West Germans, Ellen and Rolf, who we have spent quite a lot of time with. Rolf is an eye doctor, while Ellen is studying for her doctorate in mineralogy. We saw Split together, and last night Ellen cooked everyone a delicious spaghetti dinner. Fortunately, they speak English well. During dinner we talked about our respective idioms or clichés. For example, living "on a big foot" is much the same in German as our living "high off the hog." Neither of us knew how the expression got started. We hope to see them again tomorrow in Dubrovnik.

Traveling down the coast reminds us quite often of the land around the Colorado River. Hundreds of islands dot the coast, so it's almost as if we're driving along a lake or river rather than the sea. Other times the countryside comes alive with large olive groves or grapevines.

Our van is a constant source of interest to passersby, as it is a bit unusual with the pop-top and all the equipment. All day long, people walk by slowly, with several rather bold people coming right up and peering in the windows while we're inside! The most incredible incident occurred in Rijeka while we were having breakfast. A group of about ten people gathered about the car and started loudly discussing it in a foreign language. Well, we felt so conspicuous that we couldn't continue eating, so I whipped open the sliding door and we were quite suddenly "face to face." I think they were a bit apprehensive that I was upset. However, I smiled at them and for the following five minutes showed them the sink, stove, refrigerator, how we pulled out the beds, etc. They seemed quite fascinated by it all. Finally I finished the tour and said something like, "And now I go back to eating." They all smiled and thanked us for showing them the van. About three minutes after they had gone, another small group gathered around the van. Unfortunately, I had already given my limit of tours, and they had to content themselves with peering through the windows while we finished breakfast.

Split is one of the most remarkable towns we've seen. Back in the late third century AD, Emperor Diocletian built a huge palace here. When he left, the villagers just moved in and remain there today, living among the ruins! As you walk about, Roman columns and capitols are everywhere.

Yugoslavia and Bulgaria

September 10–13, 1975

September 10, 1975

8:00 p.m.
Dubrovnik, Yugoslavia

We've spent the last three days with our friends, Rolf and Ellen, seeing Dubrovnik and a few of the local attractions. Yesterday, we drove further down the coast to the small island of St. Stephan, which is a great letdown after the big buildup it was given in the guidebooks. A hotel has taken over an island about the size of a football field, and everything on the island is new but made to look old. Just to get on the island to walk around costs about a dollar per person. However, on the way we went all around the Bay of Kotor, which is very pretty.

Dubrovnik is probably the best walled city we've come across. We all circled the city on the wall ramparts and walked through its narrow streets and alleys.

Our camping site has a beautiful waterfront setting, perhaps the best we've had. However, as Ellen puts it, "The sanitaries are not too clean, even for Yugoslavian standards."

This morning, Rolf and I went swimming, and then we all went into Dubrovnik for lunch. Later we saw them off as they took the ferry to Greece.

September 12, 1975

9:00 p.m.
Sofia, Bulgaria

You may be asking, "What are we doing in Bulgaria?" Well that's a question we are asking ourselves tonight also.

Crossing the border into this country was the worst nightmare of the trip. You see, it's necessary to transfer a certain amount of money into Bulgarian leva for each day you'll be in Bulgaria—however, when I offered a lot of Yugoslavian dinars, they refused on the theory that the bills were too large in their denominations. However, they gladly took West German marks, so we're now stuck with not only too many Bulgarian leva (which is difficult to transfer back to Western currency when you leave Bulgaria), but also a lot of Yugoslavian dinars. We were really at their mercy, and I'm afraid we got the short end of the stick. The entire border-crossing episode was a hassle and took at least an hour or more—no one was even halfway friendly except for fellow travelers.

The drive to Sofia was through sparsely populated farmlands. Yugoslavia seems much better off. Very few of the Bulgarians smiled and none waved—yet these gestures were quite common in Yugoslavia. Occasionally we came across giant signs along the roadway showing the Russian hammer and sickle or Lenin.

Once in Sofia we tried to find a nice room, but all were taken. I have a sneaky suspicion that the Russian in front of us got a room, but I couldn't prove it. The remarkable thing was how very rude most people were at the tourist bureau and at the hotels. Not just to us, but to everyone. Fortunately, we found a campsite and treated ourselves to a nice dinner. Surprisingly, most people at the restaurant had glasses of Coca-Cola as their main drink! Apparently, some things never change. We had wine, lamb, salad, soup, cake, and tea for about ten dollars.

September 13, 1975

6:30 p.m.
Plovdiv, Bulgaria

In Yugoslavia, someone would have to tell you that it was a communist country. In Bulgaria, they never let you forget it. All along the roads one can see huge posters of Lenin and workers. Everything seems very dark and grim.

Before we left Sofia, Deb and I went on a shopping spree to spend our allotted leva, which we aren't allowed to take out of the country. It sounds very easy to find something for forty to fifty dollars, but it isn't in Bulgaria. Most of the stores on the street (right off the main square) were completely empty, with their windows frosted over. The other stores that were open sold food, liquor, or clothing. We went into the very largest department store we could find and saw an absolute crush of people poring over their terrible quality (although a lot of quantity) of merchandise. It looked like three times the size of Christmas rush to buy presents.

We walked the main streets for at least two hours and saw no record stores, no "mod" clothing stores, and no luxury items of any kind. The stoves on display looked like something more out of the 1930s or '40s. We found one "crystal" shop, but the quality was more like that of a dime store back in the States.

Trams and buses are packed to the brim. When they stop and open the doors, there is a regular stampede both off and on—no lines, etc., just everyone pushing his or her way on.

We finally bought a real crystal decanter in the tourist store on the main square. It turned out to have been made in Poland! If we hadn't found that, however, I think we really would have been stuck with the money, as there was nothing else to buy.

Just about everyone we meet is rude—not just to us, but to anyone. Few people smile or seem happy—most just seem to be struggling to get through with whatever they are doing. Store employees couldn't care less about helping any customer.

We took a photo of Debbie in front of a statue of Lenin.
It shows him trying to get out of town as quickly as possible.

I almost forgot to mention food stores. Some sell only bread and wine, others only meat and canned goods, etc. First you must wait in line to have someone get your can of fish or bottle of wine; then you go to another line to pay. Both lines are tremendously long, as there is usually only one cashier. Daily shopping here must take hours.

As we were driving out of Sophia, Deb said that this was the only country we've gone to where, if someone gave her money to travel but on one condition—that she stay in the country—she'd refuse to come.

Turkey

September 14—October 17, 1975

September 14, 1975

8:00 p.m.
Edirne, Turkey

We had an interesting experience on our way out of Bulgaria this morning, as I was stopped for speeding by a policeman with a baton who was standing at the side of the road. A Frenchman was stopped just before I was, and we decided that the policeman had quite a good thing going for himself. He wanted ten leva. However, with just a small protest, he decided he was a big enough fellow to forget about the whole problem for five leva.

Adding that to everything else, we shed no tears about leaving Bulgaria. Going across the border to Turkey was almost like coming home, as everyone was friendly. Our van wasn't searched, and one border guard seemed genuinely interested about what we planned to see in Turkey. When we mentioned Antalya, he brightened and said that was his hometown, but he thought it was too expensive.

We stopped in the first campsite across the border, and it's a real beauty. Everything is clean, such a pleasant change from Bulgaria. The hustle and bustle of happy people is also a nice change.

I know Deb already loves the place because the waiter at the restaurant a short walk from here helped her into and out of her seat, etc. The food was very good also, so we tipped the fellow a little over a dollar and he couldn't have thanked us more.

September 17, 1975

9:00 p.m.
Istanbul, Turkey

Although I've never been to Hong Kong, I have the distinct impression that Istanbul is the Turkish version. If you survive the trip into town, you're in for some real treats. The whole place is a beehive of activity within the old city walls. Impossible traffic jams completely tie up almost the entire bazaar area. Every other person seems to be selling something, from leather coats to mattresses. Challenging the trucks are heavily laden horse-drawn carts and stooped old men slowly marching by with hundreds of pounds of practically anything on their backs. We spent an entire day getting lost in the huge bazaar, bargaining continually, and occasionally buying something we particularly liked.

The fellows who ran the shops seemed adept at any language. One fellow even had the correct accent, depending on whether he was speaking to a New Zealander, Australian, Brit, or American! We spent quite a bit of time in one shop looking at rugs, and we later spent an enjoyable hour having tea with the owner of one of the many brass shops.

This morning we toured the famous Topkapi Palace. The treasury rooms are very impressive, and we enjoyed looking at some of the Prophet Muhammad relics such as his swords, bow, a letter, etc. We concluded our visit there by touring the harem. Then we walked to the "Blue Mosque" and watched a small part of the service being conducted. Several hundred men with small white caps sat crossed legged on rugs listening to their "minister." The women were segregated into an area several hundred feet away, and all had covered heads. The tourists were also segregated into another out-of-the-way section to watch from a distance. Except for not being allowed to wear shoes in the mosque, there were few restrictions as to how we dressed.

Next we headed for one of the two oldest Turkish baths in Istanbul, where Debbie and I treated ourselves to "the works." The men's side is completely segregated from the women's. However, from Debbie's description they must be almost identical. We both really enjoyed the experience and are probably cleaner right now than we've been in our lives. I must admit, however, that I did feel a bit strange at first having someone wash me. Sitting there next to a marble basin filled with warm water and steamy heat radiating from all over, you just about had to think about how people had been doing this very same thing for thousands of years. The only bit of anxiety I suffered was when I noticed that during the massage my 180-pound Turk attendant was standing on my back massaging me with his toes. Deb's attendant didn't do that, she says, but she must have had an interesting experience as her female attendant was topless. Deb asked if having a 180-pound fellow on my back hurt—I had to admit that it didn't—but then again, it didn't feel all that great, either.

Tonight I finished *The Source* by Michener. Although it is the second time I've read it, I found it even more fascinating this time. Perhaps seeing what he was writing about did the trick.

October 1, 1975

9:30 a.m.
Alanya, Turkey

Deb and I have been having a ball in Turkey. Almost one and a half weeks ago, we met Daver and Belgin in Ankara and have since lived like kings. We were invited out to four Turkish dinners by their relatives and were treated just like additional members of the family.

Daver's family.

In Ankara, we bought a beautiful copper tabletop and some brass pots, blouses, etc. Hopefully they will all make it home safely, but we have serious doubts about the tabletop, which is pretty large.

Often Daver worked during the day, so we read or I played chess with Daver's younger brother—a real whiz kid who hasn't lost in two years.

October 2, 1975

11:00 a.m.
Antalya, Turkey

It seems like there's never enough time to write while we're traveling. I had just begun to write yesterday when Daver walked in, and we were off again up the coast.

I forgot to mention something about our Turkish dinners—apparently in Turkey, meals are composed of several different "dishes." Poorer families, we were told, generally serve fewer than three dishes. Well, Daver and Belgin's relatives have gone all out for us, and we've been having seven-or eight-course meals every night in Ankara. They all have been extremely nice, and we actually do feel like new members of the family.

Six days ago, Daver, Belgin, Debbie, and I took off for a "vacation." We went through Konya and stopped at the Mosque of Mevlana. In the afternoon, we finally reached Kolika, near Merion on the coast. Our campsite there was incredible, as it was situated in the middle of a ruined city from the Byzantine Empire. All around us were old foundations, pillars, pieces of pottery, etc. I had the thrill of a lifetime skin-diving just off the coast as I came upon three Roman columns submerged in the water. Poking around the spot, I happened across part of an old Roman clay pot, which is now resting comfortably in the Banana. The sea had obviously risen some (or the land sank) since the Roman days, as we all later discovered the foundations of what we guessed was a palace resting just a foot below the water.

We spent two days in a nice beachfront hotel in Alanya. It had hot water, showers, etc. in each room and cost about six dollars and seventy-five cents for the two of us each night! At night, we played cards out on our little balcony looking out at the sea. As meals are very inexpensive here—four dollars for dinner for two, while lunch is half that—so we've been eating out constantly, much to Deb and Belgin's relief. Before leaving Alanya, we stopped twice—once to fix a flat tire from a small nail, and once to walk around the large castle that dominates the area, built on the top of the peninsula.

Driving here we stopped in Side for lunch and to look at the Roman ruins. Again, the area was covered with ruins and has an extremely well-preserved amphitheater.

At present we are staying a couple nights in the Hotel Antalya, which is perched on a high cliff overlooking the sea. A winding concrete staircase takes the very hardy to the water below where, again, the skin diving is excellent.

I really can't remember being so completely happy and worry-free in my entire life.

October 4, 1975

10:00 p.m.
Pamukkale, Turkey

We're staying in a hotel whose grounds surround the remains of an old Roman bath. The water is very warm, and we all enjoyed relaxing in the baths, sitting on the remains of the old columns, steps, etc., that dot the bottom of them. I felt just like a Roman and tried to imagine all of the news of the ancient world that had been discussed in this very same bath.

The Baths at Pamukkale, Turkey.

October 9, 1975

11:00 p.m.
Ankara, Turkey

Deb and I purchased a beautiful, handmade silk rug a couple of days ago and have encountered numerous difficulties trying to ship both it and our copper table home. No one told us when we purchased these items that before they can be shipped out of Turkey, they must be checked by a museum to get certification that they are not antiques. Turkish customs required receipts for both items, as well as bank statements showing that we had transferred a sufficient amount of Western money into Turkish lire to cover the cost. Since I had purchased the rug with my American Express card, I produced that receipt, only to find that customs wouldn't accept it as proof. Therefore, it was back to the bank to cash more money for the sole purpose of having a receipt! The cost to mail these two purchases, plus a few very small items, is $270!

On top of all these difficulties, on our way out of the shipping office this afternoon—our fourth trip there just today—I noticed that another car had sideswiped the Banana's driver's door and sped off without leaving a name or address! It must have been a difficult thing for the fellow to do, as I parked completely on the sidewalk—they do things the crazy way here—but he was probably an expert driver.

Turkey is in the midst of national elections, so it's been pretty exciting, as well as interesting, to sit in their capital city and watch rallies, read newspapers, and discuss the current issues such as Cyprus, the American embargo, etc. The people are a pretty excitable lot, and their campaigns thus far have reminded me more of a soccer game than an election.

October 12, 1975

11:00 p.m.
Ankara, Turkey

Yesterday afternoon we had a close call. Debbie and Belgin stayed home while Mesut (Daver's uncle), Daver, and I drove across town to pick up the Banana in the repair shop. Just after we left the house, we got stuck in a terrible traffic jam caused by the breaking up of a political rally in the nearby area. Thousands and thousands of people were marching the streets shouting and chanting. We edged our way very slowly into one of the main intersections, only to find that our way was completely blocked with people.

We grabbed some of their posters to put in the car so they would think that we were for "their" man. The crush of people around the car was incredible. We kept our windows open, as if we were unafraid because we were part of their crowd. The chanting was a roar of noise—Daver said they were saying that the present government were "killers." Suddenly a huge mob supporting the government came marching down the street toward our intersection, chanting loudly. Only a thin line of police and tanks (and our car) separated the mobs. The fellow in the car stuck behind us rushed up and said something to the effect that if we didn't get going right then, we would all be in very serious trouble.

The chanting was louder than ever—Mesut said, "Man, this is getting dangerous." The fellow from the car behind us got in front of our car and tried to get people out of our path—by now our front window was almost completely blocked by signs, slogans, etc. Finally we got through the intersection after Mesut started the car and literally bulldozed people out of the way. Within ten seconds of our "escape," a small explosion occurred where we had just left. Daver and I looked around to see hundreds of people running in all directions screaming. Mesut floored the gas and we were gone. We later learned that one person was killed and between thirty and sixty people were injured.

We picked up the van and took a giant circuitous route back to Daver's house to avoid any violence. Unfortunately, their house is only a quarter mile from where all the action was taking place, and mobs of people were streaming by when we parked.

We had just gotten inside to tell Belgin and Debbie about our close call when we heard gunfire. Like idiots, we all raced to the window to see about twenty policemen running through an adjacent lot, firing guns at unseen people. More shots rang out, and I grabbed Debbie and went into another room without windows to the street. Altogether, we heard about twenty shots. Daver's sister, Ayfer, saw the whole incident, as she lives next to the lot. When we spoke to her later, she said she had seen a policeman shoot an unarmed young man in the back of the head or neck, and that he was dragged off by the other police.

The city is very calm today. It is very difficult to believe it all happened—it came on so suddenly. Everyone is voting, and the early results show a pretty equal split between the two major parties.

October 15, 1975

7:00 p.m.
Izmir, Turkey

Saying goodbye to Daver and Belgin was difficult, but it was time to move on. The main reason we stayed so long was because our table and rug were not shipped until yesterday. We still can't believe they're finally on their way.

We left Ankara yesterday morning and spent the day driving back to Pamukkale. It made a convenient stopping point as we were both exhausted and, after soaking in the warm baths, we slept all afternoon, ate, and slept soundly until morning.

Today we climbed all over Ephesus—of St. Paul's fame—looking at the huge amphitheater, two baths, library, etc. A couple of houses still had frescoes on the walls. Walking along one of the marble streets, we saw a heart, footprint, and woman's face chiseled into one of the blocks. We couldn't figure it out, so we asked a guide later. Turns out that we had been looking at the first known advertisement for a brothel, which was just down the street in the direction of the footprint.

There's a touch of a chill in the air tonight—could winter be coming?

October 16, 1975

10:00 p.m.
Near Edremit, Turkey

We're spending an unusual night in a hotel that is completely vacant except for us. We had our choice of twenty-four rooms overlooking the sea, which is approximately a hundred yards away. The manager lives in a small house nearby, and he merely handed us a key to the front door of the hotel, showed me how to turn on the television and light the stove in the kitchen, and then left. The cost of the night was a little less than seven dollars, which isn't bad for having the run of the entire place. He told us we could use the facilities of the restaurant downstairs (which is now closed), so Debbie had a rather spacious place to cook in, compared to the Banana.

On the way here, we stopped to see the ruins at Pergamon, which were a great disappointment. Alexander the Great conquered the city in 334 BC, so it's had more than enough time to deteriorate into the shape it's in today. Later we stopped to eat in a roadside café that had some of the worst conditions we've seen, sanitary wise. There were so many flies that there was a real question as to who would actually eat the food. Why didn't we drive on? Well, we probably should have, but we had already walked into the place and it would have been a little embarrassing to leave. Besides, other people were eating there, and only half of them looked as if they were terminally ill, so we thought we had a fifty-fifty chance of survival. Tomorrow—Troy!

October 17, 1975

9:30 p.m.
Ipsala, Turkey

Troy was impressive for the feeling of history you get walking about the ruins; not for the ruins themselves, which reveal very little. Standing on the walls looking out to sea about a mile away, we could easily imagine where the Greeks must have camped, etc.

After walking around a bit, we had some tea with several other travelers and then set off for Dardanelles. The crossing was uneventful but quite exciting as we traveled on a one-car ferry. I'd never seen anything like it before. I swear that the bow of the ship came out of the water as I drove the Banana onto the back of the boat. The crossing took only five minutes, but I think from now on we'll go over the bridge at Istanbul. I think Deb's a little ashamed of the way she screamed and kicked until someone brought her a life jacket. (Just kidding.)

A fellow came by and actually tried to sell us a piece of wood from the Trojan horse! (Not kidding.)

Greece

October 18–27, 1975

October 18, 1975

8:00 p.m.
Kavala, Greece

After an easy border crossing, we took a pleasant and leisurely drive here and found a great campsite set in its own private bay and looking out toward the island of Thassos. We saw much fewer horse carts on the roads and could easily see that the average Greek is much better off than the average Turk.

It's difficult to picture Alexander the Great coming from this area, as it seems sleepy and rural. I think one of the reasons for his great success was that he conquered lands that were even sleepier.

As there is a beautiful beach in front of us and a good restaurant nearby, we think we'll spend at least another day here.

Meteora, in Greece; one of twenty-three monasteries that protected the monks during the middle ages.

October 20, 1975

9:00 p.m.
Platamon, Greece

We stopped in Philippi on our way out of Kavala. If you remember your Bible class studies, you'll know that Saint Paul taught there, founded a church there, and was also imprisoned there. Debbie almost fainted from excitement when she saw his cell. Later, St. Paul decided that the New Testament was turning out much too short and quickly sat down and drafted letters to the people there and at nearby Thessaloniki.

The forces of Antony and Octavian also defeated those of Brutus and Cassius at Philippi. The battlefield can be seen from the town ruins. Brutus killed himself after the battle; Antony went after Liz Taylor in Egypt; and Octavian eventually became the new Caesar.

Tonight we're nestled on the beach between Mount Olympus and an old Venetian castle, hoping to see Meteora tomorrow.

A few of the locals greeting the ugly American.

October 27, 1975

8:00 p.m.
Athens, Greece

We arrived in Athens by way of Meteora and Delphi. Both spots were interesting and definitely worth the trouble to visit.

Meteora consists of approximately twenty-three monasteries sitting precariously on the tops of several tall "thrusts" of granite that were formed about fifty million years ago. Apparently, during the lawless days of the Middle Ages, monks took sanctuary on top of these pillars and hauled all supplies and visitors up by ropes. Today a good road takes you up to their very doorsteps. The view was magnificent.

Delphi was interesting for its many ruins about the ancient oracle. We got a room overlooking the deep gorge and splurged by dining out in the restaurant below.

After fighting traffic in Athens for an hour, we finally were able to pull over illegally and get a map. Then it was off again to the Hotel Alma and a top floor "suite" with tub, toilet, two beds, and a large balcony with a view of the Acropolis—all for about seven dollars and thirty cents per night, including breakfast. After about a two-hour search, we were able to find an acceptable garage for the Banana.

We spent one day visiting the archaeological museum and another walking about the Acropolis and the Agora below.

We met a couple we had seen in Kavalla, Neil and Sue Miller, and talked them into coming to Egypt with us. We've accompanied them about Athens and should have a great time together in Egypt.

We all purchased our tickets from "Antonio," who is sort of a legend among young travelers. Through some sort of wizardry, he is able to send people all over the world at student rates. He's quite the wheeler-dealer and a lot of fun to watch. If any problem crops up, such as the fact that Debbie and I are not students, he smiles broadly and says, "I fix, I fix—do not worry. I am Antonio; I can do anything." Well, apparently he can, as we are all going the cut-rate.

Prices in Athens—in fact, all over Greece—are much steeper than in Turkey. We're told Egypt is very expensive—Debbie can't wait to hit that bazaar in Cairo.

Egypt

November 1–11, 1975

November 1, 1975

9:30 p.m.
Cairo, Egypt

Although our plane was delayed and we didn't arrive in Cairo until 1:30 a.m., we breezed through Egypt customs and found them all very friendly. There was no search of our luggage or any "forced" money exchange as we had been led to believe.

We all hopped into a taxi after learning the name of a clean, but cheap hotel—Hotel Tulip—and sped down deserted streets at top speed until we arrived outside the worst looking hotel we've ever seen.

As it was 2:30 a.m., no lights were on. The front door was locked but was distinguished by several broken panes of glass into which dirty pieces of cardboard had been stuffed. I rang the bell several times to no avail. Finally, the taxi driver came over and started to physically force open the door! Fortunately, the old Arab watchman arrived and took us up the elevator, where two freshly awakened clerks checked in the four of us.

Egyptian doorman.

We were all surprised to find the hotel rooms quite clean and very reasonable—six dollars and fifteen cents per night for a double with toilet, shower, and breakfasts.

It seemed as if we all should have been exhausted this morning. However, we were so keyed up about being in Cairo that after breakfast we immediately walked about four blocks to the banks of the Nile and then caught a taxi to the pyramids.

After about a half an hour's taxi ride out to the edge of the desert, we finally arrived. The taxi fare was only seventy-five cents!

The pyramids were incredible. We spent the entire day wandering about—usually pursued by a pack of Arabs who would like you to buy their Cola, ride their camel, exchange dollars for Egyptian pounds at the black-market rate, or perhaps be your guide. After a while it starts to get on your nerves, as you always just manage to give the slip to one when another fellow spots you for the first time and the whole thing begins again.

I suppose the highlight of the day was going into the largest pyramid—that of Cheops. It was nothing like I had anticipated, in that we saw no scrollwork or hieroglyphics on the walls. Tunnels leading to the queen's chamber and one leading below the pyramid to where they put the funeral boat had to be walked in a stooped position. The king's chamber is situated in the exact middle of the structure, and to reach it you must climb several ramps—one perhaps only with three feet for headspace, so again one must stoop for quite a while. The four of us went through every tunnel; and by the time we emerged from the pyramids, our legs were so wobbly that we had to sit for a half hour before walking any further. It was among the hardest physical things we've done thus far on the trip.

November 2, 1975

9:30 p.m.
Cairo, Egypt

We spent most of the day wandering about the bazaar in the "old city" and trying to catch a cab back. The bazaar was very dirty and not nearly as "civilized" as the ones we saw in Istanbul, Ankara, Alonya, etc. Filth was strewn about the roadway between the shops, flies climbed about the food in the various open-air restaurants, a huge rat lay in the middle of the road, obviously crushed the night before as it scampered across the roadway.

Cairo bazaar.

From there we walked through a large part of the city in a vain attempt to find the Mosque of Mohammad Ali. As the signs are mostly in Arabic, it's virtually impossible to find your way without help. Some drivers are helpful, but most can't speak English or read

English writing. As we walked along, we picked up a vast following of children who wanted "baksheesh"—a little money—and who constantly repeated the only English words they know—"Hello!" and "What's your name?" One little fellow, the least demanding of all, followed us for almost a mile, and just before we left him I handed him a little change. He was overjoyed, and I received the biggest smile of our trip.

Antony and Cleopatra.

We ate in a very clean Chinese restaurant that we had passed last night. Good, clean restaurants are a rarity here, and I'm sure we'll be having the majority of our meals at Fu Shings—28, Talaat Harb Street. We gorged ourselves on soup, rice, sweet and sour beef, and jasmine tea, for only about four dollars per person.

Next, we grabbed a taxi and sped off to the very impressive "Sound and Light" show at the pyramids. As the entrance fee was ridiculously high for tourists, we met a young Egyptian who led us up back alleys to a small knoll where we sat and watched the show for free. The added adventure made the show just a little more exciting for us.

November 3, 1975

10:30 p.m.
Cairo, Egypt

We spent the entire morning visiting the huge archaeological museum that is currently undergoing a vast amount of repair work. Despite that, nothing could really detract from its most prized attraction—the treasures from the tomb of King Tutankhamun. Seeing these alone would have made the trip here from Athens worthwhile. The innermost coffin (there were two others) was almost pure gold and weighed 220 pounds! We wandered about for hours, spotting things we recognized from pictures or had heard about all our lives.

Later, we walked through some of the dirtiest parts of Cairo to the main train station, where it took nearly an hour to buy four tickets to Luxor on the train tomorrow. The system they have now has a few rough edges, and we all left sort of amazed that it works at all. But it must, as we did see one train arrive while we were there.

Buses are a lot of fun to watch here. They are packed like sardines, with people literally hanging out doors and windows. When one stops, great pushing and shoving matches occur, not only between those clamoring to get on but also between them and those trying to squeeze their way off. It's really incredible.

November 7, 1975

5:00 p.m.
Luxor, Egypt

Three days ago, we caught the eleven-hour "tourist" train for the 430-mile trip down the Nile to Luxor.

Thank goodness this is not the passenger train car that takes tourists up and down the Nile. Oops! That is our train car! Think of it this way—it can only get better.

Except for being very long, the trip was uneventful—most of the time we just watched fertile fields of sugarcane, corn, etc. Occasionally we would pass an old pyramid or temple. The train stopped quite frequently, and almost every time a crowd of young Egyptian men would smilingly plant themselves outside our windows to stare in at Debbie and Sue.

November 7, 1975

While walking through the bazaar in Luxor, a young fellow offered me three hundred camels for Debbie. We all laughed—that is, until I asked how old the camels were. Honestly, it looked like it might be a pretty good deal. But OH NO; "someone" got a little upset and stomped off. As if I would ever sell Debbie. The guy did look reputable, though.

Luxor is a great deal smaller than Cairo and very dirty. There are many more horse "cabs" than auto cabs, with the resulting filth and flies in the streets. Often one sees large stagnant puddles of water that naturally breed millions of mosquitoes. Almost everyone is dressed in dirty and torn kaftans. Many people have eye cataracts or problems with their eyes. Passing children, we see that they don't even bother to shoo away the flies from their faces and eyes, so it's little wonder they have problems.

We stayed in an incredibly cheap hotel but paid a much dearer price, as Deb was bitten by bedbugs several times during the night. We immediately moved to one of the very few "luxury" hotels and reported the other hotel to the "tourist police." The policeman we met was very kind and offered us tea while I wrote out a report. He called the hotel managers, who arrived in minutes, and gave them a stern lecture and then forced them to reduce our room rent to half what they were asking. When we returned to the hotel to pick up our luggage to transfer to Hotel Luxor, we saw that two employees were busily cleaning our rooms thoroughly. Quite naturally, the quick and courteous treatment by the policeman did a great deal to calm my anger.

We've eaten all our meals in the Hotel Luxor despite the expense, as we are sure that the food is safe here. None of the food in town looks edible or clean, and there is always a cloud of flies blanketing the fruit, dates, cakes, etc.

Despite all this, nothing could detract from our visit to the Valley of the Kings across the Nile. We all rented bikes and enjoyed traveling through fields and a couple of small villages on the journey there and back. Although we appreciated the tomb of King Tut, our favorite was that of Seti I, which was enormous and completely covered with hieroglyphics.

Riding back, we went along a canal for awhile and spotted a small crocodile swimming merrily along. I took a picture of a fellow hauling water out of the canal by a centuries-old method of dipping a vessel attached to a weighted pole. I was immediately surrounded by two naked young fellows (they had been swimming in the canal) who screamed, "baksheesh, baksheesh!" until I handed them two paisters (about three and a half cents).

Traveling in Egypt is always an adventure.

November 8, 1975

11:00 p.m.
Cairo, Egypt

We spent the entire day on the train trip from Luxor. As before, nothing of great significance happened except when a porter knocked one of the connecting doors off the hinges. Everyone was reading newspapers and magazines—they were filled with photos of President Sadat with President Ford at the White House. He's been in Washington, D.C. the whole time of our trip, and apparently things went excellently. Several times people have asked Debbie and me our nationalities and smiled broadly when we said we were American. Since our relations with Egypt have just recently "warmed," we think we're in the first new wave of American tourists to visit here. The Egyptian people honestly seem to be happy to have us back.

When we arrived, our hotel room was ready for us. I had a great, hot shower, and there are clean sheets on the bed—I think I'm in heaven.

November 11, 1975

4:00 p.m.
Athens, Greece

EgyptAir has some strange hours. As it only has three flights to Athens each week, we waited until today to fly out at 6:15 a.m. Since we had to check in at 4:00 a.m., it meant that none of us got a great deal of sleep.

The flight was most beautiful, as we saw a rising sun illuminate the vast Egyptian deserts below us. Later, we flew over many of the Greek islands glowing in the first light of day. I was particularly impressed with the size of the island of Thera (or Santorini), which now sits peacefully since the violent explosion that left only the outer rim of the volcano about 1,500 BC. Someday someone may indeed discover that it holds the secret of Atlantis, or even perhaps one of the plagues of Moses in Egypt.

Crete

November 4–16, 1975

November 4, 1975

8:00 p.m.
Iraklion, Crete

After resting a couple of days in Athens, we had a "goodbye" dinner with Sue and Neil at The Stage Coach, the old western-style steakhouse in Athens. The following morning they headed out for three days in Mykonos while we waited until 6:00 p.m. and took the ferry here. It was a wonderful journey, if you enjoy screaming kids running about, no food, no sleep, and arriving at 6:30 a.m. nearly frozen to death. One rather heavy set Greek peasant woman kept us entertained by loudly snoring the whole trip. It's funny how you can get used to anything. Around 5:00 a.m., I actually stopped contemplating throwing her overboard and began to concentrate completely on the lights that were beginning to show up on the horizon.

Finally, we docked, walked about a mile to the center of town, and got a room in the Hotel El Greco, named after the artist who happened to have been born in this city. By 7:30 a.m. we were both sound asleep. We got up for lunch after we showered but found that it was 6:00 p.m.! So we altered our plans a little by having dinner instead of lunch. We've just returned and are snuggled safely under the blankets—so far Crete's been wonderful.

November 16, 1975

9:00 p.m.
Iraklion, Crete

Spent an absolutely beautiful day wandering about the reconstructed ruins of the Minoan palace at Knossos. The archaeologist, Evans, created quite a bit of controversy as he used a great deal of concrete, etc., to reconstruct the palace. Truly, we're never really sure what is old and what is new. However, we do really get a sense of what the palace must have been like before its destruction by the volcanic eruption on Thera.

We spent the rest of the day relaxing, reading about Thera, and taking naps. Both of us caught up a little on our letter writing.

Greece

November 18—December 8, 1975

November 18, 1975

9:30 p.m.
Aghios Nikolaos, Greece

We've spent the last two days in a beautiful hotel overlooking the port and bay. We've done nothing but read, work crossword puzzles, and enjoy terrific food and wine. Just read the newspaper that Stanford beat USC in football, which never fails to make me happy. With all this, it's hard to believe that we're leaving here tomorrow for Thera. I could easily just sit around here another week or so, relaxing and "living the good life."

November 20, 1975

6:30 p.m.
Thera, Greece

The trip to Thera got off to a bad start, as the ferry was about two and a half hours late. Deb and I just sat on the dock with our luggage, bracing ourselves through a violent windstorm. Because of the wind and the resulting choppy water, the ride was eight hours long, rather than the usual five. Therefore, we arrived about 9:00 p.m. in almost pitch dark and had to clamber onto a small boat that took us to the island. From that point, the fifty or sixty passengers (and all their luggage) crammed aboard a mid-sized bus that slowly took us up the cliffs on a very narrow, winding road. Finding a hotel was fairly easy, as there seem to be only three operating at this time of the year—we took the middle-priced Panorama Hotel (about six dollars and thirty cents per night) and were treated to a very nice room with hot water, shower, etc., as well as a tremendous view from the cliffs outward. We easily look down on the small island about three-quarters of a mile out, which is really the cone of a volcano that someday will grow until it encompasses the entire island again. Right now it's quite small and has had very little activity since the last lava flows about 1950, or perhaps a little earlier.

In 1500 BC, violent explosions and earthquakes left only the outer rim of the volcano. Successive eruptions have seen the creation of the two smaller islands in the middle.

This afternoon we walked down the 587 steps to the harbor, where we chartered a small boat over to the inner islands. As they are fairly "new," it was fun to walk about the huge lava flows that have hardened into rock. We saw about three craters, one still emitting hot, sulfurous steam through small holes at the northern side of the crater.

We're about to eat in the same small tavern we ate in last night. It features good, cheap food, blaring Greek music, and occasionally an energetic fellow who dances by himself to the music while his friends clap and shout their approval.

November 22, 1975

7:00 p.m.
Thera, Greece

A howling wind and a little rain have kept us pretty much indoors today except for a small foray into some of the local shops. Most of the shops are closed, as there are probably fewer than twenty tourists on the whole island.

The highlight of yesterday was visiting the Minoan ruins at Akrotiri near the southern tip of the island. Of all the ruins I've seen, these were the best in that almost everything has been left as it was found. The frescoes have been moved to Athens, but just about everything else is there—from bathtubs to huge jars—just as they were left by the Minoans fleeing the violent Thera earthquakes and eruptions.

I don't suppose there is any adequate description of the feeling one gets walking down a cobblestone road over 3,500 years old. Even more amazing is realizing that the pyramids are even 1,400 years older!

The very low doorways show that the Minoans were a very small race of people, probably five feet tall at most. The ruins show a highly developed society—some buildings have three stories. We were saddened to see the grave of Professor Marinatos, chief excavator of Akrotiri. Our guide showed us the spot where he accidentally fell and broke his neck. His widow asked that his grave be placed in "his" ruins, and you can see it in a small Minoan room next to the spot where he fell. The guide said that work on the site was discontinued after the accident last year, but plans are underway to renew the work next summer.

Twelve years ago today, our nation suffered the tragic loss of President John F. Kennedy. The memory of that loss remains as sharp and as clear today as it was then. Almost every person we have met on this trip has had only praise for his efforts. Certainly the whole world was cheated by his early passing.

November 25, 1975

10:00 p.m.
Paros

Except for a few scattered showers, the last three days have had constant rain and cold. For that reason, we've stayed pretty close to the hotel, where we've played hearts with our friends Joel and Ellen (American) and Pete and Chris (British). There isn't a great deal to do on the island anyway, so I've had a chance to finish Vincent Cronin's *Napoleon* biography. We did manage to stop in at a few shops and bought Debbie a handmade wool scarf and shawl.

November 26, 1975

9:00 p.m.
Siros

Besides catching the ferry here, we haven't done much of anything except to try to get Debbie's passport, which we happened to leave in Paros! Fortunately, we ran into a kind policeman here who phoned the police on Paros and asked them to send it along to the American Embassy in Athens. Amazingly, this is the very first time we've forgotten a passport. Naturally, we did it on an island that is reached by ferry only every three days.

December 5, 1975

9:30 p.m.
Nafplio, Greece

We stopped at one more island, Mykonos, before heading back to Athens and spending a few days doing odd jobs that have been piling up. One of the nicest jobs to have over with is mailing three very large packages home from Turkey. The Greek postal system insists on looking in each package, so one must take all the wrapping paper, scissors, etc., to the post office and wrap the contents there after inspection.

We dropped by the American Embassy to pick up Debbie's passport, only to find that it hadn't been sent yet. They were nice enough to call the tourist police in Paros and learned that they hadn't even sent it yet! It's more than a little surprising, as Paros is a small island, there are only a handful of tourists on the island now, and the tourist police just sit around reading a newspaper or drinking coffee, thinking of something to do.

We purchased tickets to fly Olympic Airlines to Israel on December 12, so we thought we would jump in the Banana and make a circle tour of the Peloponnese. We set out yesterday after a late breakfast, and both of us were happy to be on the road again. Athens has had a great deal of rain the last week, and it tends to be very depressing living in a small car after a while.

We had beautiful sunshine as we drove through Corinth and the surrounding area. We stopped at a winery and filled up our ten-litre jug with sweet wine. The other choice was retsina, which tastes a little like a pine board.

We stopped next at the ruins of Mycenae and saw the famous "Lion Gate." The huge stone blocks used in the walls were perhaps even more impressive. Best of all was walking into the domed tomb of Clytemnestra. Although it is empty now, it was still very interesting to see the way huge blocks of stone were fitted together. When we spoke loudly, the echo lasted almost four seconds.

At present we're in a small campsite right on the beach. Deb's cooking an egg breakfast, while I'm about to check the maps and propose the journey for today.

December 6, 1975

9:00 p.m.
Sparta, Greece

We've really been surprised at how beautiful the countryside has been on the Peloponnese. By far, we think it is the most striking area in all of Greece.

This morning, we hit the road early and drove all the way down to Monemvasia, on one of the two long fingers of land on the bottom of the Peloponnese. We found a spot that reminded us of both Mont St. Michel and the Rock of Gibraltar, as there is a huge mountain of rock jutting out of the sea yet connected to the mainland by a narrow causeway.

Once on the island, we parked the Banana and walked through a picturesque village. It is completely unspoiled—no postcards, curio shops, etc. Dominating the village are the remains of an old Venetian fort, which one reaches by climbing numerous steps up very steep cliffs. Deb and I wandered around the fortress for quite a while, looking at hundreds of old rock buildings that are slowly falling down, bit by bit. Little, if anything, has been done to restore the ruins except for a large church that we walked around but didn't enter. The whole time we were on the fortress, we saw absolutely no one. Before returning to Sparta, we parked on a small cliff overlooking the sea and had lunch. All in all, it was one of the most pleasant mornings we've spent on the trip. Even driving was fun, as we passed through several small villages rarely seen by outsiders and at other times had to stop while herds of sheep or goats were driven across or along the road. Quite frequently we pass villagers harvesting olives. We find it interesting that they spread out blankets beneath the tree and then pick the olives and drop them on the blankets. When the tree is completely picked they merely funnel the olives into baskets.

Just outside of Sparta, about five miles to the west, is the ancient Byzantine city of Mystras. Again, only the churches have been restored, but we spent a great afternoon walking through ancient streets among the ruins of palaces, homes, etc. We've been to so many ruins now, I'm sure we are going to have difficulty telling where some of our pictures are from. Deb wanted me to take a particular shot this afternoon, as it was a *"National Geographic"* picture. Afterward I bet her a banana split that she'd never recognize the picture when we finally see it back home. We'll see.

December 8, 1975

Olympia, Greece

On yesterday's trip to Pylos, we took the very long way and stopped off to see the remarkable caves in Duros, just a little below the Areopolis. We hadn't heard about the caves in advance but simply saw a sign advertising them by the main road. They turned out to be one of the best caves we've seen.

A winding road took us down to a beautiful inlet, where we purchased our tickets and parked the Banana. From there we walked into a tunnel leading into a wide cavern with a huge freshwater lake. Two guides take a boat of about eight tourists for almost a mile of winding passageways and caverns filled with stalactites. Although the Greek guides spoke no English, another Greek tourist did his best to keep us informed. Apparently the caverns were discovered in 1958 when a dog chased a rabbit into a hole and couldn't return. Someone went in to investigate and became the site's first tourist.

Olympia is a beautiful place among green, tree-lined hills and lush villages. The ruins are not "spectacular" but are quite interesting as, when you see them, you know you're visiting a place that has seen everyone from Alexander the Great to Nero. For fun, Deb and I walked completely around the stadium where the many competitions were held.

Tomorrow we head back to Athens to pick up Deb's passport, do a little housecleaning in the Banana, and wait impatiently for our trip to Israel.

Israel

December 12–18, 1975

December 12, 1975

8:30 p.m.
Jerusalem, Israel

Tonight we're housed in a rather large "pensione" run by the Franciscans for pilgrims visiting Jerusalem. Several, if not most, of the other guests are clergymen. As the pensione is situated in the heart of the "old city," it really adds to the atmosphere of the city, which really doesn't need much help.

We arrived at Tel Aviv after a pleasant flight on Olympic Airways and went through a very simple customs check. We walked outside and within an hour we were driving into Jerusalem in a "shared" taxi! We passed well-groomed farmlands most of the way—the Israeli Jews really have worked a miracle in the desert. Perhaps that is their strongest argument that the land should be theirs—they are the only people who have done anything with it.

As we climbed into the hills toward Jerusalem, we saw several burned-out cars and trucks at the side of the road dating from their initial war of independence.

We can't get over how small Israel is. Bethlehem is only five miles south of here. Every place is within an easy day's drive. Being prepared to fight at a moment's notice would have to be a "must" here.

Just before dinner we walked about the narrow, cobblestone streets around us. We passed people from just about every race and religion imaginable. For me, the most impressive were the old Jews from Poland, who still wear their long dark coats and large fur caps.

Some have long white beards and look as if they could be from the Wizard of Oz.

We found the church of the Holy Sepulchre amid the twinkling lights of dozens of oil lamps and candles; we walked into a very small tomb. As we understand it, there is still a bit of a debate as to where Jesus was actually entombed. But we were not disappointed even though we both expected something different. We walked for quite a while down the Via Dolorosa, the street on which Jesus carried his cross. It is truly difficult for us to believe we're here.

December 18, 1975

9:00 p.m.
Jerusalem, Israel

The last seven days have gone by very quickly. Usually, Deb and I have returned from sightseeing just in time for dinner. This was always followed by discussions over tea at the bar with other people here, leaving us pretty exhausted by the time we reached our rooms around midnight.

We took two trips out of Jerusalem: one to Nazareth and the Sea of Galilee, and the other almost down to Be'er Sheva and then over to the Dead Sea and up to Jericho.

Again, one can only be tremendously impressed at the energy of the people living here. Near Be'er Sheva we saw mile after mile of good cropland that not very long ago was desert wasteland. As the years continue and more irrigation canals are built, it should be even better.

Stopping in Arad, we saw a large new city built in the middle of the desert. At the present time, it is virtually surrounded by desert, with just the beginnings of irrigation and croplands. If we ever return, I will very much like to see how they have prospered.

Driving throughout the countryside is a real treat since we really are traveling through the Old and New Testaments. Seeing these historic spots firsthand really makes their stories come to life. For example, now having seen lush Jericho lying in the desert between the mountains of ancient Moab and Jerusalem, we begin to realize how Joshua must have felt when he drew near. He was forced to attack and defeat Jericho; otherwise, he and his people coming into "the promised land" would have had a dangerous enemy in their backyard.

New Testament stories begin to "fit together" as you see when you drive about the Sea of Galilee, the Sermon on the Mount, the multiplication of the loaves and fishes, Capernaum, Mount Tabor, etc. All are within a few miles of each other and easily within walking distance.

Personally, I think the churches have pretty well spoiled every "sacred" spot, and one today has little or no chance of seeing what a spot looked like originally. There is always a church over a tomb, on the mountain, or over the house where someone once lived. Usually they are of staggering proportions and filled with such ornate, gilded objects that after a short while it bothers you that all that money wasn't used for a better purpose.

Of all the sights in Israel, my favorite was Masada, which overlooks the Dead Sea. We took a cable car to the top and were treated to beautiful vistas in every direction. The Roman camps that seized the zealots on top of Masada for three years are still visible in the valleys below. The remains of Herod's palace at the northern tip of the rock mountain were also worth the trip.

Certainly not to be forgotten are the many interesting people we've had the opportunity of talking to here. For several nights I ate next to an Austrian who fought for Germany during WWII, was captured by the Americans on the French front, and spent the remainder of the war in a camp in Alabama. Naturally, we also met several Jordanians, Arab Christians, Arab Muslims, etc., who all have their views on the final solutions between themselves and the Jews. Believe it or not, we've even heard there is to be a small invasion of Lebanon by Israel next Tuesday to rescue Jews that are currently trapped in the Beirut fighting. Fortunately, if there is to be an invasion, we'll be safe in Athens. Originally we intended on staying here through Christmas, but Casa Nova is booked up, along with most of the other hotels. The only rooms available are about three times more than we are prepared to pay, so we decided to push on.

Deb and I both feel that Jerusalem is the most fascinating city of our trip. We've visited the Church of the Holy Sepulchre and other shrines several times. We really hate to leave tomorrow and will anxiously look forward to returning someday.

The Western Wall in Jerusalem, Israel.

Italy

December 25, 1975—January 20, 1976

December 25, 1975

9:00 p.m.
Rome, Italy

Merry Christmas! Deb and I are very thankful and happy to be here this evening. Getting here was not exactly the most fun thing we've done in awhile—in fact the last several days have been "losers."

Three days ago, we set out from Athens for Igoumenitsa in a small rainstorm. I should have known that we were beginning a rough journey, as several times violent winds nearly drove us off the roads. After driving all day, we finally arrived at the port in the dark. We tried to find a campsite, but the only one we found was closed. For that reason we just parked on the dock and tried to get a little sleep. We got just a little before 5:30 a.m. rolled around and we were forced to "rise and shine" and get in line for the ferry. For some unknown reason, customs clearance takes almost two hours before the ferry finally arrives and you're allowed to board.

The ferry ride was pleasant if we ignored several people getting violently sick during the rough passage and didn't mind being starved because the ship's pursers couldn't change any traveler's checks. As we had almost a dollar fifty of Greek money left, we splurged and bought a couple rounds of tea and a minute bag of potato chips. Since the seas were heavy, our ten-and-a-half-hour trip was extended by another hour and a half, so we landed at night.

Customs, money changing, gas coupons, etc., were a lot of fun in Brindisi. The Italian government has gone all out and hired three or four men to handle the entire operation. I'm sure it couldn't have taken us more than two hours—and I was near the front of the line.

At last we set out for Taranto to find Camping Silvana—their beautiful ad in our camping book was too enticing to pass up—plus it was open all year-round. Unfortunately, one must attempt to get through both Brindisi and then Taranto to get to the camping spot—a task that even Hannibal might have shaken his head at. Somehow, despite the traffic jams, lack of signs, incorrect signs, deviations, and road repair work, we arrived—only to find that it too was closed.

Well, we looked for a small spot to park the Banana and camped very near the beach. Neither of us likes camping this way, as there are no toilet facilities or electrical outlets, water-supply points, etc. But we made the best of it and tried to sleep while listening for thieves or strange cars approaching us.

The sun finally forced itself up, and we both looked like wrecks. Sleeping in your clothes, not shaving, etc., does that to you after awhile. We immediately searched for food and gas, as we had run out of both, and then set out for Sorrento.

The trip was uneventful until we were about five miles from Sorrento and arrived at a roadblock saying we couldn't proceed further due to a landslide. A friendly Italian showed us the nearest alternate route, which took us for the next one and a half hours up the scariest road I've ever been on. Hairpin turns for about thirty-five miles on a tiny and normally unused road that now was loaded with hundreds of Italians, all convinced they were leading the race at Monte Carlo. The view at the top of the mountain would have been tremendous if it hadn't been for the smog from Naples, which hid almost everything.

After two very near accidents, we arrived in Sorrento, and it only took three attempts to finally find our way through the town to the campsite. You see, several streets were blocked because of Christmas shoppers.

One policeman gave us directions to the campgrounds twice as we passed—in completely opposite directions. It turned out he was wrong both times, and the third way out of Sorrento proved to be the correct one. Although the campground wasn't closed, it should have been, as there was no hot water for showers, nothing clean, no food—nothing. A few good things did occur though, as I finally got a chance to shave and we both cleaned up as best we could.

Pompeii.

The following morning, putting showers on the top of the priority list, we left Sorrento and took the very windy coast road back to Salerno, then up to Pompeii to see the ruins before we camped. As Christmas was the following day, and the twenty-sixth is also a holiday in Italy, we were forced to see the ruins then. Naturally, Pompeii was tremendous, but we were disappointed to see so many of the buildings with locked doors that would only be opened by guards if you slipped them a few extra lire. It's a little disconcerting after you've already paid a high entrance fee. Also, for some crazy reason, the museum on the grounds was closed all day. On the way out, we wanted to use the restrooms but found they were locked. When I asked for the key at the admission desk, the fellow told us it was "too late" to use the restrooms, even though they were still admitting people on the grounds to see the ruins.

We jumped in the Banana and started looking for the nearest campground, as we again were almost out of gas. We stopped at a station and two attendants jumped to help us. One came to my side and tried to make small talk. But something just didn't seem right to me, so I jumped out to "stretch my legs" and wandered toward the rear just in time to see the fellow stop pumping at thirty-two litres, although we had paid for forty! Naturally I protested, but both men swore up and down that they had pumped forty litres, but they had immediately wiped the machine clear for the next customer (who hadn't even come into view yet). What could I do? I knew we'd been cheated but it was hopeless to argue further.

Very soon after that, however, we found a campsite. Both of us had a great hot shower and then just relaxed in the van. We slept well because of that, and also because the campground gate was chain-locked to dissuade thieves from entering. We woke up early this morning eager to get a start to Rome and avoid the notorious traffic jams here in Naples. Several others wanted to get early starts too; but alas, the fellow never arrived to unlock the gates! After waiting three and a half hours after the time the gates were supposed to be opened, I borrowed an Australian's hacksaw blade and within fifteen minutes we led the jailbreak and were on our way to Rome. Fortunately, traffic remained light and we found our way here without problem or accident.

As the buses are not running today, it was impossible for me to take Deb into the city for dinner, but we'll do that at our first opportunity. Over our spam, rice, and wine dinner tonight, we laughed until tears came to our eyes about how everyone at home must be saying right now "how lucky they are," etc. Actually, we know that we are tremendously fortunate, but people tend to forget a lot of the pitfalls and discomforts of traveling. I have a hunch it will take quite a while for either Debbie or me to forget.

December 30, 1975

6:00 p.m.
Rome, Italy

Today we spent "house cleaning" and showering, with a small trip into town for food. As we've walked about Rome a great deal in the last three days, we thought we deserved a day's rest.

Both of us enjoyed the forum, Mamertine prison, and the Coliseum. We spent a good two hours walking about, trying to figure out what everything was.

We spent one day touring the Vatican and still find we have to return before we leave Rome to see the things we've missed. Although it is all very immense and impressive, I find it very difficult to believe that we are in a place of worship. Thousands of people are milling about seeing the Pietà, tombs of the Popes, treasury, etc., even during services on Sunday. Neither of us feels using so much money for ornamentation is correct, so St. Peter's gave us a lot to think about. Personally, it just gave me ammunition for my arguments. If Christ ever does return, I hope he heads to the Vatican first—it should prove fairly exciting.

We did enjoy the Sistine Chapel and sat about an hour gazing up at the ceiling and front wall. Deb said that it was pretty much as she expected. However, I was again surprised at how small the chapel is.

On our outings, we always stop for lunch at small restaurants and thus far have had great success. We enjoy having an appetizer of spaghetti before the main dishes, as we never leave hungry. Also, the ice cream for dessert has been great.

Both of us still enjoy reading in our spare time. I just finished my thirty-first book of the journey—*Alive* by Piers Paul Read. It concerns the story of the crash in the Andes where sixteen survivors survived seventy days in the mountains by eating the bodies of the friends killed in the crash. After I finished, I swore to Debbie that I'd never again complain about eating spam or being cold in the van.

January 1, 1976

Rome, Italy

We spent a very pleasant evening last night, as about twelve people in the campsite built a campfire and we all stood around and gossiped the New Year in. At midnight, the sounds of fireworks reverberated through the city.

As nothing is open today, we're just sitting around reading and doing general clean-up. Just finished my thirty-second book of the trip—*The Looking Glass War* by John le Carré. I'm afraid I just don't appreciate his style.

Christmas campfire.

January 11, 1976

5:00 p.m.
Rome, Italy

Tomorrow we leave for Florence. In a way, we'll be sorry to leave Rome, as we've met some very nice fellow campers here and shared many campfires and good times.

Once, we all jumped in Brian's car and spent the day seeing the beautiful fountains at Tivoli. Another night we all headed into Rome and dined in a small restaurant. We've had a campfire every evening, so most of the world's problems have been dissected at length. Naturally, another favorite topic is travel, as we've all passed on our helpful hints to each other.

Car repairs and breakdowns have been abundant, so many an afternoon was spent discussing where to get the best value on tires and how to get at different parts of an engine. Even the Banana suffered a dead battery here. This morning we got her started again by jumper cables and ran her around a bit. Hopefully we'll have no further problems in that respect.

On the national Italian scene, the thirty-seventh government since WWII just quit. However, none of the Italians we've met seem concerned at all. On the international scene, Chou (Zhou) En Lai died yesterday after a long bout with cancer. On the American scene, Ronald Reagan is challenging President Ford in the New Hampshire primary to be held in a few weeks. Personally, I'm betting that it will be Ford against Jackson in the showdown.

January 14, 1976

7:00 p.m.
Florence, Italy

Tonight is a "stay at home and eat spaghetti in the van" night. Last night we had an especially good meal in town with another couple, Fay and Wally. It was just a small place with very friendly owners who put a gallon of wine on the table for us and served us an excellent twelve-course meal consisting of pheasant, salad, fish, etc. Many of the dishes still remain a mystery to me; however, I enjoyed them all except one. Afterwards we all headed for Vivoli's and its world-famous ice cream. Ice cream has been very good in Italy, but I think both Deb and I prefer good old American Baskin Robbins.

In the three days we've been here, we've taken in most of the sights. Florence is truly a beautiful city, and we find it much more attractive than Rome. The Duomo cathedral's façade is most impressive. We also enjoyed the Uffizi Art Museum this morning, although we were prepared to be bored by the constant religious themes. Although I can't explain it, I found it much more enjoyable and interesting than the Prado in Madrid.

We had to push the Banana to get her started in Rome for the trip here, but hopefully the battery was sufficiently charged on the journey to keep us out of trouble for awhile. I've started her every morning since then without a problem, so we're keeping our fingers crossed.

The weather has gotten noticeably colder, much to our displeasure. I think we'll really appreciate "home living" when we finally get back. I can vaguely remember how nice it was to snuggle in a nice, big, warm bed and watch a late-night movie or Johnny Carson.

Instead, we're currently being "rained on" by the condensation on the ceiling, and we've talked about how great the showers will be in the train station tomorrow morning.

January 15, 1976

9:00 p.m.
Florence, Italy

Today was spent shopping for silk scarves and ties and revisiting places a final time before pushing on to Venice tomorrow. After several smoggy days, a fresh wind sprang up this afternoon that drove the smog north and left a sparkling, beautiful city. We saw Michelangelo's *David* this morning and were quite impressed.

By the way, the showers this morning were great, although I felt they were a bit expensive at a dollar fifty per person.

Tonight I finished *The CIA and the Cult of Intelligence* by Victor Marchetti and John D. Marks. Thought it was a very valuable book; if just one-tenth of what they relate is true, we had better make some drastic cuts in the vague and ominous statutes under which the CIA operates.

January 20, 1976

4:00 p.m.
Venice, Italy

We arrived in Venice on the sixteenth and celebrated my birthday by picking up sixteen letters at American Express and then dining in a small place I had eaten at seven years ago.

It's always fun to hear what's going on at home. Apparently everyone survived Christmas without us. We also got a great bit of news as my parents confirmed that they will be flying over to meet us in Paris on February 13. We'll spend about one and a half weeks in Paris and then the same in London. Ever since my last trip to Europe, I've always had a keen desire to show it to my parents. I can't wait to see their reaction when they see the Jeu de Paume or dine in Le Procope.

Venice remains the jewel in Italy's crown that it always has been. Even the terribly cold and semi-snowy weather can't really detract you here as it might elsewhere. We've eaten out several times—nothing like fresh fish for dinner sometimes! Every morning we've passed through the open air markets and seen many varieties of fish, squid, octopus, eels, etc. Many are still alive, squirming about, so we're pretty assured that they have just been hauled out of the Adriatic.

Feeding pigeons in St. Mark's Square was a lot of fun, and we took pictures of each other being mobbed for corn kernels that you buy from a small stand in the square.

You're probably asking yourselves why I called this early morning meeting today....
Don't be rude—there are plenty of bagels to go around.

Gondolas are not much in evidence in the winter, although we did see one couple freezing to death, striving valiantly to act dreamily romantic for the benefit of the passerby.

The only problem we had was in catching the bus ride back to the campsite the first time. As we got on, I asked both the driver and fare taker if the bus went to our camping spot. Both said, "Si, si," and ushered us to our seats. Three minutes later, the fare taker came by for our tickets and discovered by looking at our previously purchased round-trip ticket that we were on the wrong bus. A few minutes later they pulled over at a bus stop and told us to wait there for the correct one. Have any clue what happened next? Yep, we waited in the freezing cold for almost one and a half hours before catching another bus back to town and beginning again. Turned out that the correct bus didn't even pass the spot where we'd been left off. So now Deb and I both have colds again, our second each in Italy.

Germany

January 22—February 8, 1976

January 22, 1976

8:00 p.m.
Munich, Germany

Deb and I are both happy about leaving Venice yesterday morning. We woke up to discover ice virtually everywhere—both inside and outside the Banana. In fact, one of our two blankets was stuck to the side of the van by a very large icicle that had formed during the night. The cold was as intense as I have ever been in. We were surprised to find Munich much warmer—still very cold, but not freezing. We find ourselves saying that staying here is a breeze compared to Venice. Yet I have a sneaky feeling that had we encountered Munich's cold weather at the beginning of the trip, we would have immediately searched for a hotel. Shows what a year on the road can do to toughen you up.

On our way here, we drove through the famous Brenner Pass and a small snowstorm—not enough to block the road, but sufficient enough to scare the wits out of anyone from California.

This morning we got up, both pleased at how warm it was, and had an egg, bread and jam, and tea breakfast before catching a bus to Munich. We arrived just in time to see the Glockenspeil work its magic over a faithful crowd of watchers. From there it was a short walk to the old Pinakothek Museum with its several Rubens, Durers, Rembrandts, Brueghels, etc.

Next we headed for the Hofbrauhaus for an excellent lunch with plenty of cold German beer. I think it was one of the best meals of the trip. We were both so stuffed that neither of us wanted dinner this evening.

I recently finished David Nivens' *The Moon Is a Balloon* and found it quite good.

January 29, 1976

11:15 a.m.
Nuremberg, Germany

Remember Rolf and Ellen? They're the German couple we met in Yugoslavia. Well, we've spent the last few days at their house in Nuremberg, seeing the sights and going out to dinner at several good restaurants. One memorable meal was venison, while last night Ellen cooked up a great batch of snails—even Debbie tried them and liked them. Rolf seemed to have a large wine cellar hidden somewhere and always appeared with a bottle of wine before, during and after.

Rolf and Ellen—It would appear that we spent a great deal of time drinking and laughing. That really isn't as accurate as…

Yesterday, both Rolf and Ellen took the day off, and we all jumped in his car and spent the day sightseeing in Bamberg. Both Debbie and I have greatly enjoyed our stay here and are looking forward to May when Rolf and Ellen are planning to visit us in San Diego. Being in a large, warm house again seems a bit like paradise after freezing in the Banana.

Okay, okay..., we probably did have a glass or two on holidays.

February 8, 1976

10:00 p.m.
Baumholder, Germany

We are spending about a week with Jerry and Kathy Brown at the military base here, trying to sell the Banana. One major says he's very interested but needs more time to think about it as well as finance a deal. Deb and I aren't very worried as it really doesn't matter a great deal whether we sell the Banana or not. If we keep her, we will have a superb vacation car that's in tip-top condition. If we sell her, though, we can avoid the expense of shipping her home.

Earlier this week, Jerry and I made a tour of the various gun ranges. I shot a fifty-caliber machine gun across a small valley at some targets shaped like men, tanks, etc. Every fifth round is a tracer, so you can see where your rounds are headed. Later, I shot forty rounds with a forty-five revolver and was shocked to see that I hit the target thirty-five times, with four bullseyes! Becky and Sheri are still the most beautiful kids I've ever seen. I've had a great time reading them stories, listening to their prayers, etc. Becky prayed one time that there could be more than one Christmas each year!

Shari, Dixie, and Becky.

Being on the military base makes you feel like you are somewhere in the United States. Everyone speaks English, and the food comes out in packages you can read and recognize. It's been a lot of fun living here and soaking up all this comfort.

The only mishap came when a water pipe broke in the church the Browns attend, due to subzero temperatures. Lonnie, the minister, called Jerry about 1:00 a.m., and we spent the next two and a half hours mopping up water.

Paris

February 12—March 7, 1976

February 12, 1976

5:00 p.m.
Paris

Yesterday we drove from Baumholder to Paris. It was very difficult saying goodbye to Jerry and Kathy, as they have become very close friends.

The interested major is still interested in the Banana, but we couldn't wait around any longer, as my folks arrive in Paris tomorrow morning. If he does finally make up his mind to buy, Jerry will write us here and we'll drive back for a couple of days.

We've secured a room in the Hotel Racine, right in the heart of the Left Bank Latin Quarter. My folks will have a nice room a couple floors below us. We can't really afford our room, but we know my folks wouldn't be crazy about a "bathroom down the hall," so we'll just spend a little more for their sakes. Another nice change is that this hotel is heated—a small difference from our last hotel in Paris.

It's nice to be back—we both love this city.

February 19, 1976

6:00 p.m.
Paris

We were right on time to meet my parents as they arrived at Orly Airport. It was quite a feat, as Orly is quite complicated and the traffic out from Paris had been heavy. When we found the TWA desk, the wind went out of our sails quickly when we learned that their flight was landing at the new Charles de Gaulle Airport on the opposite side of Paris—no specification of airport. Quite honestly, I really didn't know there was another airport besides Orly. Anyway, we quickly called the other airport and left a message to wait until we arrived, and then we dashed across town.

Naturally, as my parents were very tired from the trip, they slept through the first day. However, since then, Deb and I have made some real troopers out of them by visiting Chartres, Versailles, Malmaison, and all the sights of Paris in just six days. Except for a few things, they've done just about everything we did in a month last March.

Tomorrow, we head for Calais to cross the English Channel. I'm sure my parents will enjoy being in a country where they can communicate with people.

February 27, 1976

11:30 p.m.
London

We've spent the last week in London after a very calm channel crossing and a small stop in Canterbury to walk about the cathedral.

The major who was once interested in buying the Banana finally made up his mind not to buy it. However, by some quirk of fate, my parents happened to glance at a small ad posted on the American Express bulletin board seeking our type of vehicle. When we called, they were very interested and came by to see the van, and she now belongs to them. Deb and I are elated, as we saved the expense of shipping the Banana home, yet we were still a wee bit sad to let her go. To celebrate, we purchased a little more Waterford Crystal to add to what we bought when we were here last July.

Our forces are split somewhat, in that my folks couldn't bear staying in the type of hotel room we'd rented for them, nor could we afford the costs of a plush Hotel Russell where they are staying. Yet since the two places are within a couple blocks of each other, we just meet them in the morning at their hotel.

They have the "mouse suite." It was so named when a small furry creature made visits to their room on two successive nights. Eventually, the kitchen cat was called into the war and the enemy was immediately located. But rather than kill the mouse, the cat proceeded to play with it for the next fifteen minutes. Eventually I was able to coax a pretty exhausted mouse into a paper bag and took him across the street and let him loose in the very large park. He probably won't like his new surroundings nearly as well as the Hotel

Russell, but it's a safe bet he preferred that to the cat. So the net result was that all parties concerned were happy: My parents now have the room to themselves, and the cat had tremendous fun and will always be able to tell the other cats about the "one that got away."

Last evening, we all went to the theater to see *Happy as a Sandbag*. It was a delightful musical dealing with the WWII years in London—one of the best plays we've seen on the trip.

On the political scene in the States, Ronald Reagan and President Ford seem to have pretty well split the primary votes in Maine.

In London, the Irish Republican Army is still bombing various government buildings, hotels, and restaurants. Two explosions have gone off in the week we've been here. Many restaurants have put wire mesh over their windows to prevent the IRA from merely throwing a bomb through the windows. Apparently this has occurred several times, and business has been extremely bad for the restaurants.

March 1, 1976

9:30 p.m.
Fort Augustus (Loch Ness)

My folks wanted to make a grand tour of Great Britain, so my Dad rented a car for a week and off we went. We stopped first in Grantham to visit Harlaxton Manor and have dinner at Hop Sing's. The food was again excellent, which was quite a relief to me as I've given the place rave notices to my family for years. We spent the night at the George Hotel, which had played host to Isaac Newton and Charles Dickens, as well as English royalty.

The following morning, we drove through Lincoln to see the cathedral and then continued on to York. From there, we headed to Edinburgh, where we stayed overnight at the St. Andrew Hotel. As we've all seen the city before, we spent only a couple of hours shopping at the Scottish Craft Center on the Royal Mile this morning before driving north. Deb and I purchased eight ceramic goblets and a Scottish wall hanging. It seems that the closer we come to ending our trip, the greater our desire to buy up everything we like for shipment home. The drive today was beautiful, as the weather remains clear. We stopped in Nairn and purchased another bowl, and then drove along Loch Ness to Fort Augustus. We're in a beautiful old hotel filled with friendly people. After dinner, we returned to our rooms to find that the maid had turned down our beds and left a hot water bottle in them to warm them up for us. The woman who served us dinner told us that she fully believes that "something" is in the lake, as her grandmother once saw "it" for about five minutes long ago. Neither she nor her mother have ever seen it, but she's still hoping.

March 3, 1976

10:00 p.m.
Woodstock, Great Britain

After driving South from Loch Ness, we spent a night in Carlisle before driving here to visit Sir Winston Churchill's grave and family estate in Blenheim. Unfortunately, only the grounds were open, so we merely drove and walked about, trying to imagine what the inside of the place looks like. We're spending the night at the Bear Hotel, the nicest hotel of our trip. It is decorated with antiques and old furnishings but still has all the modern conveniences one could want.

March 6, 1976

9:30 p.m.
London

We saw Rock Hudson and Juliet Prowse star in *I Do, I Do* this afternoon. After a terribly slow beginning, it improved enough that we all enjoyed it. Neither star can really sing well, which makes you wonder why they both chose to be in a musical. However, their names are a big drawing card, and the theater is packed every night.

March 7, 1976
5:00 p.m.
London

This just can't be the end....

We can hardly believe that we fly back to Los Angeles tomorrow morning. We're flying nonstop "over the pole" on a 747, which should take us approximately eleven hours. Once in Los Angeles, we'll buy a car and spend a few weeks visiting Deb's folks in Kansas

March 7, 1976

before returning to San Diego and hopefully some type of employment. Although it will be fun to "get home," it's still rather sad to leave our European adventure. Never have I had so much fun or met as many interesting and generous people.

I've kept scrupulous accounts throughout the trip, which, for the sake of some future historical value, I'll set down here as follows:

$	975.85	Food
	1,174.90	Restaurants
	3,121.25	Clothes and gifts
	1,694.15	Shelter
	2,181.05	Transportation (gas, etc.)
	227.85	Mailing letters and packages
	920.75	Miscellaneous
	252.15	Museums
	2,864.30	Non-monthly misc. expenses such as camping gear, insurance, and plane flights to and from Europe
$	13,402.25	

We were both surprised to learn that we spent 43 percent of the time in hotels or with friends. Naturally, that means we camped only 57 percent of the time, a figure that seems a little low.

We've spent quite a bit of time this afternoon sitting in our hotel room in front of the gas heater (it's snowing outside) discussing the ups and downs of the trip. It's too difficult picking one moment as "the best," as there are far too many of them to choose from. Neither of us would choose to change any of our experiences (except maybe Debbie's Egyptian bedbug popularity), as we learned from them all.

There's really no proper way to end a story like this. To say simply that the trip is over isn't completely accurate, as it will always be a part of us. Many of the people we've met will be visiting us soon in San Diego. And who knows? We might get back to visit them again in Europe before too long.

However, Debbie and I have thought of a way we think this particular story should end. We think it should end with a hope and a prayer that we all learn to live with one another before we blow ourselves up, and that somehow all the people of all the nations will realize that we are all truly brothers and sisters.

Epilogue

It was a very different world in 1975. Most landlords would not rent to unmarried couples. Although the times "were a changing," America had still not adjusted to President Nixon's resignation or the broken promises of civil rights for all. The Vietnam War was still winding down, with frequent riots a constant reminder of how polarized our nation had become.

In many cases, if a young woman got pregnant, she would be quietly removed from school. The couple would often marry, but most of these marriages failed. I know. I was a "dissolution" attorney. I did hundreds of cases. I loved the court, personnel, the court clerks, the bailiffs, the judges, etc., but I hated the job. Somebody once said that when you're dealing with a criminal case, you see a bad person on his or her best behavior. In a dissolution case, however, you see two very nice people showing their worst behavior.

I proposed to Debbie while we were in the small fishing village of Aghios Nikolaos on the island of Crete. I woke up one morning with a feeling that something was different. Debbie was sleeping. As I watched her, I saw a beautiful, smart woman who laughed at my goofy jokes and always made me feel special. I suddenly realized this was the person I wanted to be with for the rest of my life. I was excited. I could hardly eat breakfast. I knew of a special spot where the ocean meets with a freshwater lake. Perfect place for a proposal. I walked her to that spot. She had no clue of what was about to happen. I stopped on the magic spot. I took her hand and put it next to my heart. I told her I loved her and asked her to marry me. Debbie looked at me for about five seconds and said, "It's about time!" We were married a few weeks after our return to the States.

In 1999, Governor Gray Davis appointed me to the San Diego Superior Court. After sixteen years on the bench, I joined Debbie in retirement. We have one fantastic son and a beautiful, intelligent daughter-in-law who has given us two terrific grandsons.

Debbie and I have returned to Europe approximately fifty-five times.

The Books I Read Along the Way

(Listed in the order read)

1. *The Matlock Paper*—Robert Ludlum
2. *The Onion Field*—Joseph Wambaugh
3. *The Persian Boy*—Mary Renault
4. *Eleanor and Franklin*—Joseph P. Lash
5. *The Secret of Chimneys*—Agatha Christie
6. *All the President's Men*—Bob Woodward and Carl Bernstein
7. *World Without End, Amen*—Jimmy Breslin
8. *Wilt*—Wilt Chamberlain and David Shaw
9. *Hanged at Auschwitz*—Sim Kessel
10. *The Hobbit*—J. R. R. Tolkien
11. *Harvest Home*—Thomas Tryon
12. *The Pirate*—Harold Robbins
13. *Tracy and Hepburn*—Garson Kanin
14. *Banco: The Further Adventures of Papillon*—Henri Charriere
15. *The Shadow in the Sea*—Owen John
16. *Great Expectations*—Charles Dickens
17. *The Beria Papers*—Alan Williams
18. *The Cruel Sea*—Nicholas Monsarrat
19. *The Crystal Cave: The Arthurian Saga, Book 1*—Mary Stewart
20. *Getting Even*—Woody Allen

21. *A Small Town in Germany*—John le Carré
22. *The Koran*
23. *The Source*—James Michener
24. *Bear Island*—Alistair MacLean
25. *Tai-Pan*—James Clavell
26. *The End of Atlantis*—J. V. Luce
27. *Napoleon*—Vincent Cronin
28. *Eleanor: The Years Alone*—Joseph P. Lash
29. *The Lord of the Rings*—J. R. R. Tolkien
30. *Bored of the Rings*—The Harvard Lampoon
31. *Alive*—Piers Paul Read
32. *The Looking Glass War*—John le Carré
33. *The Palace of Eternity*—Bob Shaw
34. *Harlequin*—Morris West
35. *The CIA and the Cult of Intelligence*—Victor Marchetti & John D. Marks
36. *The Moon Is a Balloon*—David Niven
37. *A Bridge Too Far: The Classic History of the Greatest Battle of World War II*—Cornelius Ryan
38. *Threepenny Novel*—Bertolt Brecht
39. *Times to Remember*—Rose Fitzgerald Kennedy
40. *The Scarlatti Inheritance*—Robert Ludlum

Made in the USA
Columbia, SC
05 November 2019